FINDING
PLAN B

FINDING
PLAN B

A Step by Step Guide on How to
Pick Up the Pieces When Life Falls Apart

TALA SHATARA

FINDING PLAN B

Copyright © 2021 by Tala Shatara

Scripture quotations marked NLT are taken from *The Holy Bible, New Living Translation*, Copyright 1996, 2004, 2015 by Tyndale House Foundation. Used by permission of Tyndale House Publishers, Inc. Carol Stream, Illinois 60188. All rights reserved

ISBN 978-1-956479-00-3

Library of Congress Control Number: 2021916860

Printed in the United States of America.

Publisher: Tala Shatara

Editor: Mallory Adamson

Cover and Interior Design: www.BookCoverDesign.us

*To my mother and father who gave me more grace,
love and support than I deserve.*

To the man who changed our plans.

To the strongest person I know, Me.

Contents

Contents

❧

"He comforts us in all our troubles so that we can comfort others. When they are troubled, we will be able to give them the same comfort God has given us."

—2 Corinthians 1:4

Introduction

Welcome, you.

The abandoned, embarrassed, and lost.

If you have washed your hair or put the slightest bit of deodorant on, then congrats, because you are already moving much faster than me in this process.

Do you find yourself not recognizing your own life? Think this is the kind of s**t that happens to everyone else but you? Do you feel empty or not whole? Are you tired of clichés like "Everything happens for a reason," "Time heals all wounds," and "There are plenty of fish in the sea?"

Then this book is for you! (said in my best late night infomercial voice)

We are searching for something together. A life of new beginnings that we never imagined for ourselves in the first place.

I know what you're thinking. You'd much rather have the Plan A you were betting on. Plan Bs have this reputation for being the second best, the "just in case" option.

Plans are tricky in my opinion. Without them, how would you get anything done? With them, you tie yourself to expectations of how things will turn out, and while you are not wrong to have those expectations, it can be earth-shattering and soul-destroying when the plans that matter most to us don't come true. We have all heard the saying, "If you want to make God laugh, tell him about your plans." It is an insightful quote, one that feels particularly true in times like these. I guess I should've titled this book *God Is Laughing His Booty Off.*

So, dear reader, what brought you here to this point?

Ending a relationship or marriage? Leaving behind a job, whether a dream or a dead-end one? Did you burn the last bag of popcorn?

I am here to help you pick up the pieces from whatever it may be. To guide you not only to find your next steps but to help you realize that you *want* to find them. I don't know about you, but in my own healing, I took more time refusing to get out of bed than actually looking for what lay ahead. I couldn't help but hold onto the old, and in doing that, I refused to let in the new. My own stubbornness led me to feel that if I didn't get my plan A, I didn't want anything else, and the longer I allowed myself to think this way, the bigger the hole I was digging for myself got—a hole of more confusion, uncertainty, and unhappiness. Months and months went by in my own life, and each day I felt as if I was getting worse and further away from my future. But oddly enough, that became the one thing that actually saved me, and it will be for you too!

The realization that I was the only person standing in my way, inhibiting myself from moving on and creating a better life, put me right back in the driver seat to keep going. To know that the longer I refused to let reality sink in, the longer I was living in an unrealistic fantasy and staying completely miserable.

I get this all sounds much easier said than done, because it is. I've been there, supremely annoyed at every well-meaning person telling me it was going to be okay and I was going to get through this. So if you're rolling your eyes right now, I do not fault you. Put the book down if you must, because not I nor anyone else can make you get back up again. You are the only person who can get yourself to start over.

Starting over.

Geez! It pains me just to write those words.

It is painful enough to re-route a simple aspect of your life, but to completely go back to square one is *terrifying*. But that is why I am here to help you pick up the pieces, because doing it alone is not an option anymore. You and I know what it is like to lose something so special, and that was our plans. Whether that be a breakup, divorce, losing a job, and/or failing at anything you have worked so hard towards, your life has ground to a halt. Everything that you dreamt and worked for has crashed and burned, and it can be very hard to come back from that.

I know this feeling all too well

After 23 years of being bullied, disappointed and let down in my hometown, I finally picked up and left to start over in one of the best places on the planet—Nashville!

I knew it was time to get out and finally cultivate relationships with more like-minded people. No more fake friends, no more dead-end loves, and no more haters. I was on a mission to create my own destiny, to go out and get what everyone else around me had. Plan A.

While being in Music City, I soon found a loyal girl squad, got an amazing job in the music industry, and was finally surrounded by people who were cheering me on rather than tearing me down! I was living my best life. Nothing could make that life even better.

Enter *him*.

We met at work and instantly caught each other's eyes. Who would've thought that the workplace could be more than timesheets and horrible break room coffee?

He resembled a real life Clark Kent from his appearance to his demeanor. Every day he showed up in a freshly steamed button up and studious Ray Ban reading glasses, but behind the professional facade I found a man I had been dreaming about but never laid eyes on before. Until then.

Once those glasses came off, GQ magazine came out. His Polo cologne and gorgeous big brown eyes had me falling hard. I remember it like it was just yesterday, first seeing him next to the water fountains on that musky 5th floor. It was love at first sight, and I knew that happily ever after was just over the horizon. And since everything else in my Nashville life had magically fallen into place, I knew that this would too.

After dating for a short three months, we moved in together and took life by storm. As time went by, our discussions went from "What's for dinner?" to "How many people should we invite to the wedding?" This was it. I'd found my forever person, home, job, and *life*. I finally felt what it was like to have the perfect life that all my friends and social media feeds had.

Over the years, we lived, laughed, and loved. The memories

we created are still, to this day, some of my favorite moments in life thus far.

However, you know what they say, nothing lasts forever, and in just a blink of an eye everything went from pure bliss to the exact opposite.

Even now, I really cannot tell you exactly what went wrong. Maybe it's because my brain is blocking out the trauma, or maybe I was creating a false reality of what was actually going on in our household. All I know is, my life changed forever.

My plan A consisted of marrying the love of my life, moving into the gorgeous home we built, and having lots and lots of babies! When he disappeared, so did my plans.

This all happened in the year 2020. Ever heard of it? The year of this little thing called the *coronavirus*. I bet you are still reading this while wearing a mask right now, because let's face it, this is here to stay. If you have been living in the woods on a spiritual retreat, with no cell service or WIFI for the last year and a half, then you might need to Google some things. I swear they will dedicate college courses to the year 2020. Heck, even toddlers will learn those numbers before the alphabet. If you don't know, there is/was a global pandemic that swept the planet, resulting in lots of deaths, work from home orders, and to-go alcoholic beverages. If that doesn't sound crazy, I don't want to know what you think is. Consequently, everyone had to quarantine for months due to the pandemic.

Quarantining in a shoebox apartment with the love of my life? Sign me up! Our days consisted of working from home, laughing, movies, pranks, cooking, etc. All the good things! I could do this forever. But that changed when we actually started feeling like it *would* be forever. I am the most extroverted extrovert you will ever meet. Have a wall? I will talk to it. For someone who thrives off human interaction, the isolation started to take a toll on me. As for him, he loved it. If he didn't have to see another human being ever again, he wouldn't. That is when everything changed. The reason he loved the isolation is because it enabled him to do the things that society wouldn't accept. He drank heavily and became addicted to marijuana, in the kind of way that, if he ran out, he would become edgy and lash out. Every day, he was more and more becoming a completely different man. I tried so hard to help, but I was suffering from depression and, really, you can't help someone who doesn't want to help themselves. In this time, we immaturely decided to build a home. Silly me for thinking that a new house would make all of our problems go away, but I was desperate to stay optimistic.

Ultimately, all the promises and shiny new countertops in the world weren't going to save us.

Towards the end of the relationship, my battle wounds were starting to show. My friends and family started to take notice of the change in my demeanor. It soon became hard for me to be around my friends and their significant others, because I was constantly being reminded of the differences between a happy, healthy, loving relationship and what I was living in.

By that point, I had lived enough to know what I wanted and how I wanted to be treated. I have gone through my own struggles in the past that have taught me all that I value and deserve. It was time to put those past lessons to the test, and make the hardest decision I ever had—to leave.

Leave the man I thought was the love of my life, my home, my job, my friends, my city, my *life.*

In leaving him, I had to leave it all behind. His being was attached to everything my life consisted of in Nashville. I couldn't work without seeing his face, I couldn't spend time with friends without being constantly reminded of him, and I certainly couldn't sleep another night in the home we'd shared.

With the constant triggers, I left Nashville and returned to my hometown. It wasn't until the first morning I woke up in my childhood bedroom when I truly realized my whole life had changed.

I want to be very clear, this book is not for the dumper or dumped, for those terms don't matter when it is all said and done. There is also this misconception that the dumper doesn't feel any pain, because that is simply untrue. I can assure you, I am feeling much more pain than him. Fast forward to a week after we broke up, and he was already trying to enjoy company of other women. *That was fun.*

I mean I guess this was to be expected. According to the *New York Post*, divorce rates in America increased 34% during the COVID-19 pandemic due to the economic, psychological, and social challenges it presented. It stinks learning that you've become part of a really sad statistic. But I'm not just a number in a news article. I'm a whole person who already had a fair share of prior trauma before any of this crap happened. In the end, I was so close to the end zone. I could see the finish line where all of my hopes, dreams, and countless prayers waited for me. When my race was stopped short, I felt every inch of pain, sadness, depression, anger, and all the horrible emotions you can think of. It wasn't pretty, and, in being truly vulnerable with you, I almost didn't make it out.

I am here to be that person in your life to ensure you don't fall into that trap.

#NoWomanLeftBehind

Our stories don't have to be similar, but I believe our pain is very much so. We not only lost something significant, we *lost*. Defeat has replaced normality and hope. I don't know what could be more traumatic than losing everything. Losing your hopes, dreams, plans, goals, can be everything sometimes. I mean who are we without those things anyways?

I guess it is time to figure that out now.

CHAPTER 1

Expectation
vs. Reality

L et's talk expectations.

All the hopes, dreams, visions, late night discussions, blood, sweat, and tears.

Now let's talk about what really happens.

Pain, shame, regret, doubt, discouragement, depression, anger, confusion, pain... The list could go on much longer.

With the effects of Covid-19, we have all had to change our expectations to some capacity, but sometimes it takes just one more change of plans to push you over the edge. If you've lost way more than you have ever experienced before, you may not know where to start when it comes to picking the pieces back up. I sure didn't.

I grew up learning that whatever you aspire to be or have in life would all come true with determination, passion, hard work, and prayer. If you want to own a Mercedes Benz, it was achievable. If you want to be the president of a company, or even the United States, it was possible. But what if you want to be a wife or mom? What if your happy ending stems from something intangible such as love?

Society has conditioned us to believe that we must not be standup women if we don't end up with the husband, house, and babies. So, when reality takes away those expectations, it is incredibly derailing because of what they mean to us as women.

For me, I lost my sense of self, who I thought I was *meant* to be.

One of my all-time favorite movies is *Legally Blonde*, and, considering my age, gender, and great sense of fashion, it is no surprise why!

I was catching a re-run on TV the other night when something stuck out to me for the first time, which was very telling since I had seen this movie at least a hundred times.

If you have not been graced by this cinematic gold, allow me to explain. *Legally Blonde* is about a woman named Elle Woods, who decides to go to Harvard Law School in hopes to appear more serious and win her ex-boyfriend back. This movie is filled with legal jargon, study groups, sexual assault in the workplace, and a riveting murder trial, so pretty much as realistic as it gets in this day and age.

As Elle was preparing to embark on her law school journey, she first met with her academic advisor to discuss her next steps.

"Harvard Law School?" her advisor said. You can imagine her confusion as Elle Woods is a Fashion Merchandising major with little to no previous interest in the U.S. legal system. Although Elle had a 4.0 GPA and was the president of her sorority, her advisor was still in shock, and it showed.

This was the moment I had noticed something I never had before.

"What are your backups?" her advisor asked.

Backups, another way of saying Plan B, wouldn't you think?

What was her Plan B if she didn't get into Harvard? What was her backup plan if she failed miserably in law school? What other options were there if she ended up hating it? Her advisor wasn't wrong to ask this, but it seemed she forgot she was in a movie, where everything goes right!

That is when Elle confidently answered, *"I don't need back-ups, I am going to Harvard."*

For the first time, that scene became more moving to me than it ever has.

I'd like to think we all are the same way when it comes to our plans. We don't have our minds set on something with another one tucked away in an "if all else fails" kind of way. How much love and dedication would we really have for our goal if we had another plan in our back pocket? Would that be the sensible thing to do? Or do we go into WWEWD (What Would Elle Woods Do?) mode—have one plan and fight to ensure that it's fulfilled no matter what?

After all, movies like these are meant to inspire us. I cannot tell you how many of my friends went to law school and became successful attorneys all because of that movie.

#WhatLikeItsHard?

However, since we aren't living in a movie, do we need to consider the more realistic alternative? Are we acting unprepared since our plans are not guaranteed? To have the understanding that plans aren't promised and learn to suffice with whatever path you go on? When we lose a life we wanted so bad, can it cause us to take the more cautious route the next time around?

I can see it now, if Elle Woods was a real person, she would post an Instagram picture with the caption reading *Expectation vs. Reality*. The first frame would be her acceptance letter to Harvard, and the second picture would show Elle going out to the neighborhood bar getting wasted every night as a law school dropout.

Thinking about this expectation vs. reality mindset really got me thinking about what expectationss can do to us. Expectations turn into hopes, and hopes turn into dreams, and the next thing you know you are daydreaming of a life that could be extremely far from reality. And that is what we start holding onto. The false reality.

There have been many moments in my life where I have been let down immensely, because of my own false realities. Whether a failed relationship or friendship, to even as little as getting my dinner plans canceled, are feelings I know all too well.

This feeling that you are going through now is equivalent to getting all ready to go out, when a friend tells you they cannot go anymore, only a gazillion times worse.

I used to have a boyfriend who constantly stood me up. At the time, being a young high school girl, it seemed natural to keep falling into the trap every time. I would get all dolled up, ready to have a fun evening, but then fast forward to hours later, I was sitting at the restaurant alone, continuously calling a *blocked* number. After the 7th time of this type of treatment, I finally started to catch on. With the countless apologies and coincidental emergencies that kept popping up, I knew I was being taken on a heartless ride. It wasn't until the 8th time he asked me out that I knew what was on the other end of that night. I remember still saying that I would be there, knowing actually I would be sitting on my bed with no makeup and my pajamas on. I had no expectations and knew to expect only the worst when it came to him. Afterwards, getting asked out on a date by him was just another way of saying I would be staying home that night. And unfortunately, it did a lot of damage to my self-esteem in the long run.

Being stood up all those times made me feel like I was destined to have this happen for the rest of eternity. Every guy that shows any interest and asks me out will ultimately do the same thing—abandon me. Being let down and left in the dust too many times can make our expectations shift drastically. Usually expectations are exceedingly higher than what we may or may not see actually play out, but how do we live when our expectations are actually worse? To know that any future plans we have are not envisioned in an enthusiastic kind of way, but rather a dreadful one?

I became a pessimist by default, and my brain rewired to believe that being hopeful was a load of crap. Soon after every time a guy asked me out on a date, my first thought became, "Let's see how long it takes him to cancel."

And while disappointment happens to all of us, the message from the universe I received each time was to lower my expectations. I swear, the more I have lived, the more I have been given advice essentially to have very little faith in our world, which, if you ask me, is a horrible way to live.

Nowadays, we cannot talk about potential boyfriends, jobs, vacations, etc., without being constantly reminded that what we are dreaming about has a high chance of never even happening. Having low expectations is pretty much the same to having bad expectations, so it seems as if everyone is encouraging us to be negative. You can imagine what kind of pessimistic human beings we can easily become if we stop believing that all the good things we want in life will eventually crash and burn.

I can assure you that my expectations were not at all what I lived. And while I knew that with some time things would get better, I was hesitant to go out into the real world again for a long time because of this message in my head. I was unable to see the beginning without automatically seeing the end attached to it. With the typical disbelief and stubbornness of not getting what I planned for also affecting me, I was inhibiting myself from not only healing but even *wanting* to heal. When our plans don't go the way we want them to, we can be affected for years to come.

Because we are beautifully flawed human beings dealing everyday with other beautifully flawed human beings, so much is bound to go wrong. However, what doesn't make it easier is when we live these hopes and dreams within our minds before they play out in the real world. You and your mind have already determined what will become of your dreams. Who will be there, what will be said, and everything in between has already been real within the most powerful place—your brain.

I am here to bridge the unknown world of reality and fantasy. They say dream but don't dream too big. Have high hopes, but not too high. So it is time we find the happy medium when we slip into the mysterious world of hopes and dreams. The higher your expectations, the higher the cliff you stand on looking down to see how things will play out. When they go terribly wrong, the harder you fall. I am here to help you become a dreamer while still remaining a realist. In other words, I want you to dream *real* dreams.

With all the rubble and darkness, I am here to get you through life after the destruction and keep your outlook as clear as can be.

Living in a way where you strive for the best is powerful. It can give you a sense of determination and drive to achieve it all. However, when life doesn't play out the way you planned, it can rob you of the joy and the feeling to ever want success in the future, which is the exact opposite of what needs to be happening in your life right now. Keeping the faith is the most important thing you need to hold onto during this time, and, honestly, your faith should be taken care of before anything else. After all, why try looking for Plan B, if you don't have any hope it is even out there?

I am saying this because I want to challenge you to stay as optimistic as you were before the event that led you to this book. I don't want your life to get permanently derailed by the situation at hand. I don't want you to start believing that you should always take the cautious route. I don't believe we should teach ourselves to settle and assume that our expectations are not feasible. As I've gotten older, I realized the most important thing in life is to believe. Not only to believe in our plans but to believe in ourselves—**to have faith that, even if things do not work out the way we thought, we will always have ourselves to fall back on.**

I feel that we are the only people to make our expectations our reality. It just takes getting back up and trying again, with new, more honest (and ultimately better for us) expectations. Don't allow yourself to believe that what you truly want is not what you will receive. That is what this journey is all about.

CHAPTER 2

Ugh, God

*W*hy me?

I bet that is a thought you have had many times since your Plan A said *sayonara*.

I cannot tell you the number of times I have rolled my eyes to Heaven, wanting to shake my fists and cry out these words. Amidst everything I was going through, which was already hard enough to come to terms with, it was *really hard* to admit that I was outrageously pissed off at God.

Before I go on, I want to address why I decided to discuss this. Throughout this book, I am going to talk about God a lot, because I truly believe that faith in Him is essential to picking up the pieces and finding our Plan B. That being said, when we are hurting and confused, it is completely natural to feel angry and resentful that we are going through something so awful. So I am going to tell you something that maybe no one has ever said to you before. *Let yourself be mad at God.* This is as real as it gets, y'all. What you are facing right now is no joke. The ugly, dark, and difficult world that brought you here...well, it sucks. I am not going to sugarcoat anything, but what I do hope is that what I am about to say will make you feel understood.

Ugh, God.

How many times have you been told that God will never give you more than you can handle? So, in this season, why does it feel He *has* given us more than we can handle?

God said He would never forsake us, but I bet you feel pretty forsaken right now. God said He would never leave, but you might feel completely alone. God said He would provide, but you feel somewhat empty handed. God said He would not allow you to be burdened with more than you can bear, but now you are at your wits' end.

I know.

Because I was there too.

I thought I knew God until my world stopped. Turns out, in my darkest moments, He was almost the last person I wanted to speak to. I resented Him for what had occurred in my life, and I was confused as to why He would deprive me of what I had been longing for—a husband, a home, a family. Why did I lose the things that, to me, make life worth living? I couldn't fathom that I was brought into this world to feel completely abandoned. I guess this is where the Christian in me would say, "God puts us through tests so we can cling onto him tighter." And the rest of me would say, "Yeah Tala, you're right. But how long do I keep that up?"

Truth is, we all get burnt out holding onto God's promises, especially when it seems things keep getting worse rather than better.

After losing the life I wanted, I moved back home to find anything that would give me hope again. While I was on that path, I was still being bombarded with some of life's worst challenges.

Shortly after I returned to my hometown, I got laid off from my job. Since jobs were very scarce due to the pandemic, getting hired was harder than ever. I was met with constant rejection, slammed doors, and one-liners such as, *Although we were impressed with your skills and qualifications, we have decided to move forward with another applicant.* It was exhausting, and, quite honestly, it made me doubt myself and never want to apply for anything else ever again.

During this, I was also losing friends left and right. Whether for good reasons or not, everywhere I turned people kept disappearing. The world kept getting lonelier, and still I was expected to "keep the faith."

They say when it rains, it pours, and I had definitely been in a monsoon for quite some time. While I was losing all that mattered the most to me, I was also losing my grip holding onto God.

Ok so what? I lost my boyfriend and the plans we had together. *Hold onto God.*

Ok so what? I lost my job and financial security. *Hold onto God.*

Ok so what? I lost everything. HECK NO! GOD WHERE U AT???!!!

Life seems so unfair that we have forgotten that life was

never promised to be fair in the first place. In times like these, it's easy to dig ourselves deeper into the "not fair" hole by comparing ourselves to the ones who do seem to have been dealt a pretty fair hand. You know the ones. The ones who got it all on the first try. The ones who will never truly relate to you and your struggles. The ones that will look at this book in bookstores and wonder "what the heck is a Plan B?"

It is tough being surrounded by that, for if that is all we know, we expect our lives to go in the same, easy direction as theirs did. I feel the most prevalent feeling we have had in this journey so far is an emotion we are ashamed to even admit we have, and that is jealousy. We are jealous of the ones who will never have to experience something as destructive as this, and who is to blame for that?

If we are being honest and vulnerable here, we shifted the blame to the One who created all our lives. And that is God Himself.

Why, God?

If God created all things, then did He create my downfall and someone else's success? Is He the one to be held in contempt for my life being the exact opposite of what I want and deserve, since He is in the driver seat?

In this being a Christian book, it might seem odd that I am

discussing hating on our Savior. However, being happy with God all the time is not what being a good Christian is all about. We are human, and God created us as such—to feel like humans, to think like humans, to react like humans. Being completely content 100% of the time is unfeasible and beyond any Christian's capabilities. So no, it is not wrong to be frustrated at Him in this process.

It's also not wrong to be frustrated with the people who do their best to persuade us to believe this all happened for a greater picture.

"God knows what He is doing."

"This was all in God's plan."

I swear, every time someone says this to me, I picture a scene in my head of God tied up with his mouth duct-taped shut, while the devil is controlling our lives, driving them into the ground.

insert evil laugh

Because, if I am being honest, how on Earth is God's plan for us to completely rip away all of our hopes and dreams? To

do away with our plans and remove all things in life that make us
us? It has to be someone else taking over, for God would never
do such a thing. Or would he?

This all gets me thinking of the story of Job.

Job was a man who did everything in the name of God. He
was a righteous man, and he was blessed beyond belief by God.
He had it all—a beautiful wife, kids, servants, cattle, land, good
health, and more! For all his abundance, he lived in gratitude to
God, the One who provided him with the fruitful life he had.

During an encounter with Satan, God praised Job as being an ultimate servant of His and a man of ultimate faith and
devotion. Satan had a lot to say about that and proposed if God
would take all his fortunes away, Job would not lean on Him in
the same way. To prove the devil wrong, God removes all the
good in Job's life by killing off his children and his livestock, de-
pleting his land, and damaging his health.

Job got to keep his wife, but she really wasn't happy about
their new lot and she let Job know it.

Despite all Job's loss, he still rejoiced in the name of the
Lord and became fully content with his circumstances.

I came naked from my mother's womb, and I will be naked when I leave. The LORD gave me what I had, and the LORD has taken it away. Praise the name of the LORD!" (Job 1:21)

Job was determined to find peace in his suffering, even though the ones around him didn't understand why. His own wife pleaded with him to curse God and throw all of his hope and faith away. But he never did.

Soon after this, Job's friends came to visit him after they heard of his misfortunes. As they sat with him, they couldn't believe what Job was going through. One by one, they offered up a reason why this all happened to Job. To them, there had to be a logical explanation God would allow one to suffer so badly. They started to create a list of hypothetical sins Job must have committed. His friends became adamant that Job must have done something wrong to be dealt such a horrible card. But Job assured them he hadn't done anything. Soon after, his friends believed that Job was being punished for being too proud to admit he had done something wrong. But again, Job shut down their accusations and got very angry at their pointing fingers.

It wasn't long before Job lost all that he knew and ultimately started to view God as being reckless, unfair, and corrupt. He then demanded God come down and defend His reasoning behind his suffering.

I cry to you, O God, but you don't answer. I stand before you, but you don't even look. You have become cruel toward me. You use your power to persecute me. You throw me into the whirlwind and destroy me in the storm. (Job 30:20-22)

Soon, a whirlwind of a storm cloud shows up and, what do you know, it is God!

God showed Job all things He created and asked Job to know He is the only One who will understand these things.

He told Job that even all that is bad and evil in the world has still been created to be a part of His good world. All of this is through His wisdom. God wanted Job to know that all He creates is complex and by clinging close to Him all understanding will be found.

After discussing with Job why all this has happened, God then restored all that Job lost and even provided double what he had before. But that isn't the end.

The end of this story is what actually matters the most.

Job went on to become a man who praised God on the good and bad days. No matter what God threw his way, he trusted in God's wisdom for understanding.

The End.

I love this story for many reasons. First and foremost, we are actually able to identify in scripture what suffering looks like. I sometimes forget that the Bible is not only full of the happy, fruitful, and inspiring, but can also depict what pain and distress look like too. Sometimes being able to relate back to scripture can help us understand that even the most faithful people were also persecuted without cause.

This story also teaches us to be mindful about when we praise God. Are we doing so when we are living comfortably and abundantly? Or do we need to start practicing on understanding our Lord when things go awry too? I believe that is something we as a world need to do better about. I have to admit, I used to be the type of "Christian" who only reached out to God when it was convenient for me. I was a stranger to God because I only came around very few times. Sometimes it feels wrong to be mad at God for when things go wrong, because we only show up for Him when they do. God does not want to only be revered when things are going right. He also does not want to be revered only when you need something. Your devotion to Him should be continuous. If it is not—that is ok. It is now the time to start introducing God to all of you and not just parts of you.

Another reason that particularly sticks out to me in the story of Job, was the role his wife played. Some people might wonder why God removed all of Job's sources of happiness, but still left him his wife. I believe Job's wife, let's call her Karen, represents that part of us that is furious with God for putting us through what is happening in our lives right now. Karen persuades Job to believe God is only a good God when our lives are full of blessings and make total and complete sense to us. As things kept getting worse in Job's life, she begged him to give God a piece of his mind! Karen told Job he must be angry at God, for God is to blame for all the misfortune Job has gone through. We can admit it, part of us has thought the same thing. But Karen is not the star of this story, and neither is that part of us. God created us to be like Job. So, when we get angry at God, we don't need to curse Him and blame Him. Instead, we should cry out to Him, draw closer to Him, and lean on his understanding and wisdom.

Thankfully, the story of Job does, in fact, end on a good note, and I believe there is another lesson to take away from that. In the end, this is all happening because of a greater picture that hasn't been unveiled. Yes, yes, yes, just like those people said. The thing is, we are just in the awkward beginning stage of this process, letting skepticism and doubt take over. But thankfully, we have a great depiction of suffering and what that means to God.

In my opinion, the Bible is meant for interpretation. That is what makes scripture so beautiful. Each of us can read the same stories, psalms, verses, and all experience a different feeling. We all can take away different messages from the same story, and that is exactly why we have this awesome tool to rely on! No one should tell you what you should be taking away from these stories. It is all about what you feel scripture is saying to you.

In the Book of Job, I am sure we each found something that stuck out to us.

You might be wondering if the reason this all happened was due to Satan's suggestion that we only obey the Lord when we He provides. "*Was this a test to see if I still remain faithful when I'm not favored?*"

Maybe you are starting to think like Job's friends, who were adamant he was due some misfortune. "*Did I do something in my life to have deserved this?*"

I know what it's like to feel God has created me only to forget about me. I've spent countless hours screaming up at the sky wondering why He would stay so silent while I live in a very loud and discordant world. In times like this, I not only have questioned my own situation but all the terrible things going on in the world. Global pandemics. Cancer. Homelessness. Suicide. You and I are not the only ones to look up at the sky and question why. This world is full of questions. Yes, much like Job, we are angry with God. We might still have questions that have gone unanswered and struggle with a faith that is more fragile than glass. That is the feeling of Ugh, God.

God knows we have questions, and even more so, He knows we are extremely upset with Him. That is why I love the Book of Job. This story leaves us with an abundance of messages to take away when we talk about suffering, and here is what I believe they are. (Remember, you might have you own!)

God does not owe us any answers for His actions.

Keep your faith and understanding on God.

Never allow anyone to alter your understanding of God.

Believe all things will all work out because of His wisdom.

This might not seem like the best news you want to hear, and I am sorry to tell you that the answer as to why God allows us to suffer is still very undetermined. We honesty will never know during our existence, unless we have died and come back to life. You better believe I will be asking Him all of this the second I get to Heaven! I am writing this to let you know your frustration with God isn't going without notice and it is very much acceptable, even if it feels completely inappropriate.

You might still feel like Karen. That's ok. Or maybe you're more where Job's friends were, asking what you could have done to deserve what's happened to you. Whatever you're feeling, this story shows that you are not alone. It also shows you that there is a way to move forward. Don't let your pain destroy your faith or paralyze you. Be angry at God if you need to, but don't pull away from Him. He does have your back, and He will show you that.

Your Ugh, God will soon turn into Thank you, God.

CHAPTER 3

The "C" Word

I *need to get out of this place...*

...is the first thought I wake up to these days. My latest predicament has caused me to sell my apartment, the one I shared with *him*, move back home, and live with—yes—my parents.

Oh, how I love experiencing the feeling that I'm going backwards in life and having someone dictate what I do and what I say. Or rather, what I *don't* do and say.

No more McDonald's runs at midnight because who's to know? No more raising the TV volume above 15, because I *finally* can. No more sleeping in because I simply feel like it.

No more freedom.

Don't get me wrong, I am so fortunate to have the parents I have. Having a place to stay when my whole world has come crashing down has been such a blessing, one I know not everyone has. The emotional, physical, and financial support that they have given me is incredible. However, it is the simple event of waking up in my old bed every morning that is a constant reminder that EVERYTHING has changed.

My mind is working overtime. I am constantly thinking about what is next. I have always been the type of person to know what I want: to chase the dream and to never let anyone get in my way. Even in this time, it is still in my blood to think about what is next, to answer a simple question: What now?

In my situation, I have found it to be completely out of the question to move back to Nashville, the place where I fell in love, built a home, dreamt of a life, planned for that life, and watched it all come crashing down. That city was my Rome. I built it up and watched it fall without a warning. You would be surprised how a big city like Nashville can seem so small when something like that happens to you.

The home I built with my future husband stands there. I still hadn't even seen it when I left. My life, hopes, and dreams are there. My future baby is there.

I keep having this vision of hearing someone say "Congrats Tala, it's a girl!" as the nurses and doctors walk away with my newborn and hand her into the arms of another woman standing next to *him*.

With all the baggage Nashville carries for me, I cannot return. How can someone start Plan B, while A is still staring them in the face?

As I started thinking of my next path, I kept being haunted by something.

Poké Bowls.

There is this place in Nashville that makes the best poké bowls. All the fish, toppings, and sauces you can imagine! I ate it for every meal for weeks! I got it when I was happy, sad, anxious, and every other emotion there is. It was my comfort food for sure. And I cannot help but wonder, what if my next destination doesn't offer this new Hawaiian/Japanese hybrid delicacy? What if they do and the taste isn't "just like home"?

This is the era of the "C" word.

Change.

When people tell me they like change, I immediately A. hate their guts and B. think they're lying through their teeth. How can someone be so undisturbed in a world where things could change with or without any warning?

"Oh NBD, my husband left me. It's cool!"

"Oh NBD, I got fired, but it's fiiiiiine."

Oh man those people really get me going. The people that come across as so placid and unbothered no matter what life-altering events are happening. But they are on to something.

Upon further investigation into these calm and infuriating individuals, I've found there is a reason they remain content when life starts to spin out for them. The "C" word that puts to shame all the trials and tribulations of Change.

Christ.

Change is no match for Christ.

Most of the time, when we experience change, it feels unpleasant. I mean, it's never a good thing when the lady in Google Maps suddenly and unexpectedly says Rerouting... Having to deal with change is having to re-route your plans. But the Google lady is just doing her job behind the scenes. Whether you, as the driver, want to believe it or not, she knows more than you. It took me a very long time to realize that a change in plans is *God hard at work*.

But how do we learn to lean on Christ in the face of Change?

If you're anything like me, losing your Plan A can make you feel like your world is out of control. Like sand slipping through your fingers or standing in one of those windy money vaults unable to catch a single dollar. The thought of that machine gives me anxiety.

You might feel your body is paralyzed, unable to move forward, refusing to take one more step through the life you did not choose first. Your stubborn bone has kicked in. Don't get me wrong. Being headstrong is great, unless it is forbidding you from living the life you were meant to live...in the eyes of God.

Your Plan B awaits with the One who created your second option before your first.

Knowing this, how could we not find a world of relief knowing that this was all pre-meditated? If God knows what your life has in store for you the way he knows how many hairs you have on your head, it almost takes the element of surprise away. This change of course that you have gone through is not new to God. In fact, he knew it before you were even born. Thinking about this has helped me transform my pain into peace. God wants me to draw near Him, and He wants the same from you as well.

God sends us on winding roads hoping we will seek him out through the twist and turns. But what does it mean to seek him out? Is it as simple as prayer, or do we need to get baptized in the Jordan River to really show our acknowledgment and devotion towards Him?

All I know is the first step is to believe. Believe that every-thing and anything that has happened so far in your life is all a part of a bigger picture. And best of all, to believe you are not going through this alone.

First and foremost, if you do not feel Jesus around you right now, rest assured He is there. I can't tell you how many times I have sat expecting to "feel something" to know that Christ was present with me, only to feel worse than I already did when my deepest senses didn't tingle. So, if you feel like it is taking you a while to find that connection, be patient with Him and with yourself.

You see, for me, being forced to go to church at a very young age did the exact opposite of what my parents were in-tending. I never understood who the "Big Man upstairs" was or what he was trying to do *for* me. I struggled with anxiety and depression most of my life, and after my world came crashing down, I wanted desperately to be free of them once and for all. I'd tried everything (or so I thought): medication, therapy, meditation, essential oils, exercise, etc... all great things...but completely short term fixes for me. The one thing I never tried was PRAYER. I was convinced there was no way connecting with Someone I could not hear or see would help me with what I was going through.

I know how alone you feel right now, and it seems no one is saying anything that is helping you in the slightest bit. But what if the right answer isn't spoken but still can be heard?

That is the power of Jesus, for He can reveal more to you than anyone possibly could. It all starts with the power of prayer.

I think there is a misconception with prayer, meaning it needs to be as formal as possible. As if you are at the Royal Wedding or something.

"O most loving Jesus, the wonderful ... O Jesus, Thou the beauty art of Angel worlds above, please deliver me from the waters that I am drowning beneath, and bless it thy neighbors in every passing, to which they feast in joy and peace."

Give me a break.

God does *not* want us to be scared of speaking to him. He wants us to be comfortable and relaxed so that we can open our hearts to him and feel his presence. Don't worry whenever you cannot get the words out; God already knows what is on your mind and in your heart.

"...for your Father knows what you need before you ask him." *(NLT, Matthew 6:8).*

I kid you not, the first time I prayed I was like, "Hey there J. Listen I am hurting right now, and I would really love it if that could, *like*, stop. Please and thanks!"

Once I realized I can pray in my own voice, it completely stuck. So, if you did not major in Praying 101, no sweat. I got you covered.

I urge you to stop reading at this moment, and, wherever you are, say out loud or silently these words or whatever pops into your head: *Dear God, I am not ok. Please take care of me. Please heal my heart. Please take this weight off me and allow me to breathe easy. Allow me to feel that something bigger than myself is carrying me. I choose to trust you, Lord. And when I seem like I am straying away, please hang in there with me. I'm new to all this. Amen.*

God knows the changes we will go through. He knows the good, the bad, and the ugly. He knows everything your life will contain. He even knew you would be reading this at this very moment.

Knowing that God is in control of this scary change we're going through, that old cliché actually means something. Everything does happen for a reason, and that reason has already been determined by Christ.

Now when I encounter one "C" word, I automatically think of the other. Anytime I get low, depressed, angry, confused, and lost, I chant "Change = Christ."

New home? Christ. Eviction? Christ.

Happy marriage? Christ. Nasty divorce? Christ.

Pregnancy? Christ. Miscarriage? Christ.

Job promotion? Christ. Being let go? Christ.

It reminds me that change is greater than myself, and whether it feels good or bad, it all was created by Christ, who has already seen the future. It brings a sense of comfort knowing that there is a blueprint of my life that remains with Him.

Change does not need to be understood, but Christ does. God wants us to understand that any form of change in our life is not only planned by Him but meant for a bigger intention. Whether God is replacing what we have lost with something better or He wants us to simply call on Him, we are all due some sort of modifications in our lives.

Change teaches us that nothing is guaranteed except God's

love and promises.

Christ has guaranteed us an abundance of blessings.

Whether or not it feels like it right now, *change is one of them.*

CHAPTER 4

~~Love~~ Validate Yourself

As I was walking my own journey to find Plan B, I found myself talking with one of my good friends about her own recent breakup. She and her boyfriend had just ended their five-month relationship. She was devastated, and rightfully so (he ended it via text message). After she got done telling me all that went wrong, I offered up my advice. Considering I was also still in a state of post-breakup turmoil, I was definitely not equipped to provide anything useful to ease her pain.

It was like the blind leading the blind.

Even though by then my mind was basically a museum of the inspirational and motivational quotes people kept spouting at me, I really couldn't think of anything I could say to help the situation.

But then something popped into my mind that I *had* to get off my chest *immediately*.

So I said, "Well, just be grateful you weren't together for longer, living with the guy, building a home together, and having to move cities to get away from it all."

Right when I said those words, I felt the way other "misfortunate" people talk me through similar moments. It was bittersweet to say these things.

On one hand, it felt strangely good to prove that somebody else's situation wasn't as bad as *mine*. On the other, I'd become one of those people who has "one-up" another person's misery. I really don't know why I said that to her, because I know exactly what it feels like. Loads of people did the exact same thing to me when I tried to open up to them about my experience. Instead of acknowledging what I was feeling, they'd give me the "at leasts" and the "you think that's bads," using my grief as an excuse to tell their own sob stories and leaving me feeling completely exposed and invalidated. Now I'd just done that to one of my friends.

That's when I realized the importance of feeling validated in our feelings.

If we don't feel validated, we tend to act out. We almost make our life worse by sulking and refusing to let go, so that we can finally get the attention we crave and have satisfaction for proving we have hit rock bottom.

After my breakup, I felt like I was drowning in everyone else's idea of how I should be feeling. I guess I sort of did that to myself. Unlike many, I don't shut people out when I go through a tough situation. I always feel that I need guidance when it comes to my own feelings, and I am ready to include my closest friends into the regular tragedies. The problem is that I am never satisfied with any advice I get. My friends are always either too blunt, taking emotion out of the conversation, or they're too nice, sugarcoating in the most obvious way just telling me what I want to hear.

During one of my weekly "my world has fallen apart" kind of breakdowns, I decided to call two of my good friends for some emotional release.

The topic of these phone calls was an extremely tough session I had in therapy that morning. If you haven't had much time in therapy, I highly recommend it to anyone who might be against it. If you have done therapy, I think you will relate to what I am about to say.

Therapy is tough! Of course, it can be a safe place that harbors you at your most vulnerable times, but sometimes you have to open up hard conversations. And when this happens, it can be really difficult to stuff those feelings back into the box when your 53 minutes are up.

Inconveniently, you might be dealing with the fallout for the remainder of the week until your next session.

Hopefully this isn't scaring you skeptics out of giving therapy a try! It's worth it, I swear.

As I was on the phone with my friends, I explained I wasn't in a good place due to a heavy therapy session, which had left me feeling burnt out.

Friend X was sort of distant. She really didn't give me time to air out my emotions and was almost rushing me off the phone. To give her the benefit of the doubt, Friend X had never had much experience going through anything tough to really relate to this kind of issue, and what came out of her mouth next really showed that.

She said, *"Well, if therapy does that to you, maybe you should just quit therapy."*

Even though I knew she said that because she didn't "get it," I still felt completed invalidated. Needless to say, I don't call that friend anymore in these situations.

But then along came Friend Y. She was a friend that actually had been through something extremely similar in her life. If I was going to listen to anyone's advice, it would be hers every time. She had experience with therapy, so she knew exactly how I felt. However, she took understanding to a whole other level.

She said, *"Tala, I feel so bad. You will have a level of PTSD for the rest of your life because of all you went through."*

Not sure if I felt better or worse after that phone call.

Those two extreme opposite phone calls taught me two things. 1. I needed to start leaning on myself, and 2. If you are going to offer any words in a time like this, "I'm sorry" will do.

When people pass away, it is customary to say, "I am sorry for your loss." I think these words of comfort can be applied to all types of loss and grief. Telling someone who is grieving that you are sorry might seem small to you, but it can be monumental in terms of healing for them. Saying you are sorry for their loss shows that you acknowledge what has happened. Telling someone you are sorry can do many things.

It is the perfect phrase for someone to know you feel their grief. It also allows you to say something that makes the other person feel you aren't trying to change the circumstances they are under.

No matter what or how many times someone offers up their best advice, the circumstances aren't going to change, so, in my experience, having someone talk in circles about how things will get better just prolonged the hurt.

I even got to the point that I told people who were constantly trying to fix me to just say they are sorry. I know that the people around me are just hurting just seeing me in pain, but in their efforts to speed up my recovery, they were doing more harm than good.

I will never forget the day my best friend looked at me and said, "So you just want me to tell you I am sorry your life sucks?" It was most definitely a weird request, but it was the only phrase that helped me. It was a phrase that said, "I hear you," "I validate you," "I understand you," and "I care about you," all in one! It was honestly just what I needed to help me start to heal myself all on my own.

We cannot begin to take any steps forward without giving ourselves some much needed validation and steering clear of people who invalidate us. Get rid of the idea that you are not worthy of being understood!

As women, we are constantly searching for approval in everything we say, do, and wear. My actions do have a purpose, but most of the time it is to be noticed for something good. We not only want to receive approval when the world is going right, but especially when the world is going wrong. We have turned everything into a competition, and by the end of it all we are playing the game of Who's Life Sucks More? But funny enough, we don't even realize we are participating in this competition because we didn't actually agree to play! Regardless, it seems we strive to have the most when it comes to success and wealth and in having the *best worst* stories too.

We have this subconscious belief that if we do in fact have the worst life, we will be attended to more often and can heal quicker. I think that is why we crave validation from comparing ourselves to others. If I have it worse, then you obviously have to take care of me; therefore, the more you take care of me, the faster I will recover. We want everyone to drop what they are doing and everything they are going through to attend to our needs, and by doing that we will be on our feet in no time. At least that was the case for me.

What I didn't understand before was that to validate someone is to do more than just give them your approval of their feelings. It is monumental and can drastically change the way a person views not only their situation but themselves too. I always believed the best medicine in this world was laughter, but as I have gone through life and have experienced more downs than ups, more no's than yes's, I've learned that validation is truly what can save the day.

Putting yourself and your feelings first is how you truly begin to love yourself. When we validate our own emotions, we are saying that we will do no matter what to ensure we remain safe, healthy, and happy.

I believe the ability to validate another person's feelings is a form of emotional intelligence (EQ). Validation comes from one of the most important characteristics of EQ—empathy. Empathy allows us to read the room, so to speak. It is an awareness of other's feelings and emotions. According to the International Journal of Caring Sciences, Empathy includes valuable skills that enhance our attitude towards others and ourselves. These skills include controlling impulsive behaviors, increasing patience, regulating mood fluctuations, and inhibiting frustrations towards ourselves and others. To master this kind form of intelligence is extremely pivotal when dealing with our own emotions that could easily cause us to take the destructive way out.

Having empathy allows your mind to understand the possibilities of what could be going on behind closed doors before you react. Knowing we are all going through something makes it so much easier to empathize with people in their darkest moments. Mastering this skill means you have more patience and understanding not only for others but for yourself!

My ability to self-validate did not happen overnight. When you hear one too many times that what you are going through is *not that bad*, you almost start to believe it. You can easily believe you are just a dramatic person who enjoys sulking to get attention. However, negating those thoughts is the first step to validating yourself! There isn't a step-by-step formula on how to respect your own emotions, but I can tell you that not allowing yourself to believe those lies is part of it. Unfortunately, most of the people I've met, at least, were not taught the skill of empathy in school. I really hope someone is putting that on the curriculum these days. That means we have to become stronger advocates for our own emotions, since we might not be getting it, even from the ones who love us the most. Good and bad emotions all have a place in this world. We are allowed to create space for all of our thoughts and experiences, to recognize all our emotions and give them the respect they deserve. If you are sad, there is a legitimate reason. If you are angry, it is important that you discover why. If you are happy, hold onto that feeling and let it take over. Allow each emotion that you possess to live out into its' entirety. Don't push any of them away. Process them, respect them, understand them, and *validate* them.

They say the first step toward recovery is to admit that there is a problem, which is the essence of validation. I cannot even begin to tell you what refusing to admit that I was in a dark place did to me. I was paralyzed by the thought that my life went from sunshine to darkness in a matter of 24 hours. I wasn't releasing the feelings that were staying bottled up, and in that I was enabling myself to feel let down and broken.

I've noticed time and time again that validation helps us heal quicker. If we do not get validation for our troubles, we prolong our recovery. We either spend more time persuading others to validate us, or we completely lose the will to move on.

In moving on and finding your Plan B, the first step is obvious—love yourself.

They say you cannot love anything or anybody else until you have completely fallen in love with yourself.

If you asked me before my whole world came crashing down if I loved myself, I would have undoubtedly said yes. It wasn't until I was left all alone in the debris of the destruction and incapable of standing on my own two feet that I learned I actually had no idea who I actually was.

On top of it all, I have now figured out I am subject to major self-esteem issues, body dysmorphia, and the self-confidence of Eeyore the donkey. Being tied up in a very toxic world revealed that I was not putting my emotional and physical health first. I had more issues than Vogue, y'all!

A couple months into my new reality, I decided to join a dating app to help me move on. Oh, how these dating apps have changed over the years. Forgive me, but it has been a long time since I have been on one. You can now put your political affiliations, religion, and even your preferred pronouns on there! Talk about progressive. I have to say, I learned way more than I wanted to know about some of these guys.

Being on this app for about a week, I concluded that dating

SUCKS, and I would honestly be better off dying alone than even attempting to go back into the unpredictable dark hole of dating. I cannot tell if these apps are making it easier to find love or actually way harder.

Through my short time swiping, men came and went. Some were great, and their mothers should be proud. But I soon realized I was spending more time paying attention to these men than to myself. Two months in, I decided to delete the app and start swiping right on myself.

I believe we should be madly in love with ourselves, but I really had no idea where to start. Is it as simple as saying, "I love myself," or do I have to go further and get that phrase tattooed on my body?

I also wonder why when women, in particular, go through a breakup or divorce, the first item on the to do list is to love yourself? Is there some sort of unspoken rule that you cannot commit to yourself while in a committed relationship? Do the majority of women not love themselves with a significant other? I needed to figure out why this was so common.

I was in a state where I have given so much of me to someone that threw me away, I did not even recognize myself. I could barely make decisions, big or small. The thought of making one more decision, only to find out later it was the wrong one, yet again, was enough to send me into a nervous breakdown. Eating in or going out? Friends or The Office? Applebee's or Ruby Tuesday's? What if I chose Applebee's in hopes they still have that amazing chocolate cake, only to get there and find out they are sold out?

I couldn't choose!

After all, you saw what happened the last time I made a choice.

After thinking over my newfound indecisiveness, I started to realize that this new habit of mine was merely a mask as to what I was really feeling.

I felt like a house with cracked foundation that stood perfectly fine until a tornado came through. I knew I'd lost everything external in my life; I hadn't realized I'd also lost my foundation. If you are wondering whether or not you might have the same problem, getting easily derailed is a good identifier. So, if you get just as anxious about small life decisions or bumps in the road, your foundation might be caving in.

I was crumbling and nothing and no one could catch me. In the end, there was only one choice to make. I had to catch myself.

Strong foundations are what make us built for this life. Without them, we are unstable, unreliable, and unfit to care for other people, let alone ourselves.

Every day, we are adding more cement blocks to our structure. In how we were raised, our life experiences, and lessons we have learned along the way, we are constantly under construction. However, when a devastating experience comes in like a wrecking ball, we could, *unintentionally*, erase all of our hard work instantly. And I believe, to an extent, you and I might have done that.

We've watched our metaphorical home fall. However, I am so happy to remember that, even though we might feel homeless, we always have a safe place to go. God has opened His doors for us and is waiting for us to come inside.

He has welcomed us in so that we take the time to build our foundation not only to its' original form but even stronger. We are in God's home getting rest, taking stock, and figuring out what our next steps should be. This is the time to rely on God, to speak with Him and create a game plan that includes Him. What this has meant to me is that anywhere we go physically, we are still in His home. Coffee house, gym, work, gas station? We are constantly moving, but so is God. He is traveling with us, protecting His children at all times. Keep reminding yourself that you are never alone, and when things become tough, escape to His home in your mind. I created a hypothetical image of what that looks like. If I am ever feeling lost or burdened, I go to His home in my mind.

I imagine myself sitting in God's living room next to His warm fireplace. We sit and discuss that I feel as if my peace has been tampered with, and I need to get back to a grounded level. Pretty much anything that is creating an uncomfortable feeling in my body gets spoken about to Him. Think of God's metaphorical home as a paradise rehabilitation center. It is full of all the resources you need to become a better child of His every day. It is abundant with love, understanding, peace, and, you guessed it, validation! This has helped me tremendously when going about my days. Sometimes we get caught up in the fast life with work, family, friends, etc., and anytime I need to slow down, I remember that I am safe with Him. He loves and validates me, which brings me a sense of peace each time and every time.

As we find our Plan B, we are in a state of revival, and knowing that we will never be alone during this process has been the most comforting token I have been holding onto. Our situations might be very different, but we are united in pain. Everyone goes through different battles, but no one's pain is greater than someone else's. Different, maybe, but not more or less important. If someone who has not experienced your circumstances or does not feel grief the same way you feel it, don't judge them for it or get angry at them for not understanding. And definitely don't let their reactions make you feel like your trauma is invalid.

Your trauma is valid even if:

There are others who have experienced something worse.

It happened a long time ago.

You did it to yourself.

Someone doesn't understand it.

Writing this book had many purposes for me, but I knew the most important one was to validate you, reader. Some people just won't get it, and it can relay through their words to you. We can't change the way other people respond to our pain, but we can become emotionally aware that we all have been put through different struggles in our lives, and these shape us all in different ways.

I validate your struggles, girlfriend. I am here for you.

CHAPTER 5

Slow Down

I will soon be 25 in a couple of months, and although I have yet to find a gray hair, I feel so old!

Back when I was building a life with someone, about to be moving into our dream home we built, I felt like 25 was the perfect age. It was the perfect time to get married and have kids without people thinking I was too young or too old.

Now, I am in such a rush it is not even funny. Every guy I see in passing or come in contact with, I immediately think is possibly *the one.*

Just this morning, I was batting my eyelashes at the Starbucks drive thru barista while he handed me my drink. He gave me this smoldering, relaxed look that seemed like he was feeling the vibe I was putting out. It all seemed right until he said, "Did you need something else?" which completely snapped me out of the fantasy I had just made up in my head.

Guess I will have to wait a little longer for the Starbucks barista of my dreams.

Unfortunately, I am not a patient person. I refuse to wait in lines or be put on hold, and let's just say if someone takes too long to tell a story, I am already checked out. As a woman, I am constantly reminded that time is ticking. Women have no time to lose. We have to be *on it* when it comes to career, love, babies, and money. The longer we wait, our selection of men deplete just as fast as our fertility. The media, science, and our mothers are constantly in our ears, telling us to *hurry up*.

In my own life, I am surrounded by happy endings. Currently, my two best friends are pregnant, and my other best friend is engaged. It doesn't take a board-certified psychiatrist to understand how brutal it can be to be surrounded by all these beautifully successful Plan As. Of course, I am extremely happy for all my friends' happiness, but the more I'm around it, the more I want to change my own situation.

Sound familiar?

The feeling of standing still while everyone else is gracing through life can cause you to push on the gas even harder, fearing you will soon miss your own chance to achieve the same milestones. Not feeling as accomplished in your personal or professional life can cause embarrassment, self-resentment, and even a little bit of FOMO. We are the only ones in the driver seat, right? It has to be up to us to gain all of our accomplishments we have planned for, isn't that correct?

Holding myself as the one who could be the only one to provide success for myself, I started to feel the pressure that I created creeping into my mind every day. I soon became almost afraid to have happiness, because if I didn't achieve the life I wanted, I would be the one to blame. I became distracted by my own fears and insecurities. At the same time, I couldn't let go of what I wanted. Who will hold my plans safe and secure better than me? Who will guard my dreams and keep them unharmed? Who will ultimately provide the things that I aspire to have and want to be?

In this being a Christian book and all, it is pretty obvious who... Jesus, duh!

For headstrong people like me, it is very hard to surrender to Jesus, even though He has promised to keep our most sacred hopes and dreams safe with Him. He acts as a tarp at the bottom of a very high cliff, and yet we still contemplate whether we want to take the risk of being caught by Him at all. Casting all your anxieties onto Him sounds easy, but there is a reason we all struggle to give him our burdens. We cannot bear to be that vulnerable, putting all of our trust in Him, because we have convinced ourselves we can only function when we are in control. That's why letting go and letting God is one of the hardest things I ever had to learn.

We are taught to put our emotions on Him, for he will take the weight off our shoulders and put it on His, but why do we insist on keeping on doing this all alone? Have we as humans become so untrusting that we would rather continue on with the sleepless nights and worrisome minds than fully surrendering our distress to the Lord? I believe the majority of us have. When was the last time you were listening to someone venting about a problem they were facing only to end the conversation with "I have put it in God's hands, and know I will be taken care of?"

It doesn't make us bad people to not acknowledge God's promises and give him total control; it makes us human, and thankfully He knows that. But if we start a habitual pattern of slowing down, we can break the cycle.

By slowing down, we can teach our minds not to forcefully take control when it doesn't need to. In doing so, we learn to act more appropriately, make clear and thought-out decisions and judgements, and let things naturally fall into place.

You know the story. Don't rush while driving to your destination. You'll get a ticket, or something far much worse. It's better to get there safe than sorry. The same analogy applies here.

A sense of urgency in finding the right path can cause your car to spin off the road. You might even end up with a bigger mess on your hands than if you actually trust the process.

Allow me to elaborate.

There are 2 types of women in this situation. One woman is still crying herself to sleep, feeling every inch of pain, unaware of how and when her first steps to go on will be. The other woman has decided to put all the stress, anger, and sadness into a shiny new next step, to conquer and succeed.

Which woman is more stable and successfully finding her Plan B?

Is it the woman who suddenly has no hope to go on, never feeling the need to get out of bed? Or is it the woman who dove into the deep end so she could feel a sense of gratification in all her hurt and pain?

I would argue the woman in bed has more stability and sense of reality than the other. Of course, the other has a great sense of empowerment and drive, but her race to the finish line has voided her ability to grieve and ultimately make her own true choices. By trying to avoid her pain, she's letting herself be controlled by it.

I have to admit, in my own journey, I have had to constantly remind myself to slow down. My own attempt to race to the finish line came a month after my life fell apart. I am not one to sit idle. I hate down time and always have to keep busy to prevent my mind going down a dark hole. I needed to find what was next. I told myself that the day I would finally be "ok" is the same day my better life would come along.

I told my dad that I wanted to open a women's clothing boutique. I came to him with this fantastic idea in my mind and a commercial property for rent in my hand. This was it! I was going to put all the anger and sadness into this store and make it the best this town has ever seen! This was for sure going to keep me busy, and I would be getting over *him* in no time with this new project.

There was just one problem.

I forgot I had no money.

After that, it was a PR firm. Soon after that, it was an ice-cream shop, and the list of my great new business plans went on and on for weeks.

It finally took my dad sitting me down and voicing these words I will never forget: *You can't learn to swim while drowning.*

All of a sudden, reality started creeping back in. Holy s**t! I am sad, not well, and completely broken. I can't do all of this, surely not right now. Not in this capacity. Who am I to think all my problems would go away with opening up a business, with money I did not have, managing several people working for me, while trying to stay afloat during a pandemic?!

Although it brought back the heartache, this reality check also introduced me to something that changed the way I thought when I got too ahead of myself.

I finally understood what patience really meant. Patience is an accessory to the word *trust*.

To trust God is in the driver's seat, and that he would never let your car spin out.

Girlfriend, you and I have been demoted to the backseat.

I believe this is the most important message I can share

with you. You will not be able to succeed in this journey without trusting Him. If you want to shut this book now, I would be okay with that. If this is all you can take from this, I feel accomplished.

You might be asking, what does it mean to trust God? Is it just the act of saying it or do we need to prove it? I believe we all have different ideas of what trusting God really means, and because of this I decided to do my own homework. I gathered a couple definitions from some of the closest people in my life to see what trusting God really meant to them.

Here are a couple of the answers I received:

1. *Putting my faith in God, not leaning on my own understanding. Admitting that I can't do it on my own.*
2. *Regardless of my will, hope or understanding, God knows what's in my best interest and is the ultimate sovereign power in my life. No matter what I may suffer (because even suffering can lead to future prosperity for myself or future generations), I have an eternal relationship and a place in heaven thanks to the gift of Jesus.*

I encourage you to really find out what trusting God means to you. There are no wrong answers.

In thinking of putting faith into the unknown, I started to really unpack what that meant, and in doing so, a new thought stopped me in my tracks: Why are we so willing to trust in the unknown, without any hesitation, but when it comes to trusting our Lord, we hesitate?

In most cases, we are taught to trust in the things that we cannot hear, see, or prove. In that, I started to wonder why we have an accepted sort of gullible behavior.

Who here can prove that Abraham Lincoln was assassinated by John-Wilkes Booth at the theatre? I wasn't there, and I am sure you probably weren't either. All that we have are our schoolteachers lessons and illustrations of what historians "believed" it would have looked like. What about the Boston Tea Party? Evolution? Cleopatra? Aliens?

Now before you call me a conspiracist, I am merely trying to show you that the act of believing without seeing is something you are already quite good at.

We have been using trust as a sort of sixth sense all our lives. Somedays it still gets tough having to trust in a higher power, but I always remember that trusting is a skill we have had since the beginning of our existence. This whole time we have been taking an eyewitness's word that's been passed down like a game of Telephone without any uncertainty, but we still have trouble trusting the One who made all the creations these eye-witnesses, well, witnessed. So, if it ever feels hard to put your trust in God, just remember this is an artistry that you have been mastering for a long time.

I hope this conveys how I truly feel about trusting. It has to come from within. You cannot trust with your eyes, ears, arms, legs, or lips. Only with your heart. Your soul will feel a sense of relief once you fully surrender your worries and anxieties to Him. We don't know the outcome of what God will do in our lives, but we must trust that he will take care of us no matter what.

Do you remember the things you lost up to this point? A love? A job? A friend? A life? Losing these things can cause you to lose something much more impactful—faith. Losing faith is essentially losing your religion, your happiness, your optimism, and, worst of all, *yourself*. Holding onto faith in this time is hard, and you will be put to the test to see how long your grip can hold.

I have one friend who went through a very similar situation to mine. After being with her boyfriend for almost eight years, they had a child and got engaged. To make the long story short, he turned out to be not the one for her, and they called off their engagement just weeks before the wedding. She ultimately picked up with her son, moved to Nashville, and started over. When you talk to her, she is always happy. Her smile fills the room, and she never speaks badly about anyone. Even with experiencing a huge loss, she has become such a positive soul. I asked her how she is so happy after going through something very traumatic, and also how does she make finding what is next look so effortless?

Her answer—faith and patience.

When she said that, it all made sense. Even though other people have been trying to tell me that very same thing. I think we can all agree that it is much easier to identify with people who have gone through something similar to you. No one listens to the girl who got everything she ever wanted on the first try. And trust me, I have plenty of people in my life like that too.

All in all, what I'm saying is *slow down, girl!* Sometimes the longer you take to heal, the stronger you become.

Not to mention people literally do anything for you when you're not 100%. LOL!

But in all seriousness, it took me so long to figure out that slowing down actually sped up other things. Taking things day by day allows you to think more clearly. You won't know what you want if your mind is distracted by a million other things. Don't let outsiders influence what you should be doing and how long it "should" take to get better. Time is ticking in our minds, but trust is flourishing in our hearts. The more you watch the time pass, the more it passes you by. I encourage you to completely throw your mental clock out of the window. You will be happy you did.

CHAPTER 6

The Only Way Out Is Through

I remember this one time I was at the OB/GYN for an annual checkup and was completely dreading it. With my monumental fear of doctors' offices, the uncertainties of what they *could* find, and, well, the uncomfortable, torturous-not-actually-torturous thing we are actually there for, it felt like enough to send me into cardiac arrest.

Most young girls ask their moms to go with them to scary doctor appointments; however, taking my mom to this one might just be a case of TMI. So, I asked my best friend Lily to go with me.

Lily is the lesser dramatic half of our dynamic duo, so she

is naturally the best person to keep me calm in very not calm moments.

We were sitting there waiting for the doctor to come in. Lily was sitting on the extra chair in the room scrolling through SnapChat, while I, on the other hand, was sweating profusely, telling myself that not only is this going to be very uncomfortable, but that there is a good chance they are going to find some incurable disease down there. Not because I'd done anything to contract an incurable disease, but, you know, *anxiety*.

The doctor finally walked in all smiles. For someone who deals with *that* part of the body all day, she was exceptionally chirpy.

"You ready?" she asked.

I was seconds away from throwing up and passing out all at the same time. I was ready to bolt and head straight to the car and never look back.

Lily knew I was on edge. I mean, why would a self-respecting woman ask her friend to hold her hand during a routine checkup? I was heading into a full-blown panic attack as I started to back away from the doctor who was getting ready to *insert*.

Lily took my hand and stared me down.

"You are doing this. You are already here, so the only way for it to end is to get it over with," she said.

I'm not sure if it was the great pep talk or the scary girl yelling at me, squeezing my hand so hard it could fall off, that got me to shut my mouth, sit back, drop my knees, and, well, you know the rest.

Thinking about the situation I am in now, although it doesn't involve doctors, and screaming best friends, it still compares.

In Lily's words, we've got to "get it over with." Another way of saying "the only way out is through."

If we start thinking that way more often, imagine all that we could get done.

We can stand in line for hours at the DMV, sit through uncomfortable flights, take hard tests, do mundane chores all around the house, and even get through the fears of going to the doctor.

We can soon realize that everything will pass once we actually pass through it.

It makes me think about perseverance and what God says about that. In scripture, there are stories after stories symbolizing the overcoming of adversities and pushing through a storm.

It was through the Red Sea that God led His people out of slavery. It was through the desert that He molded and shaped a generation primed for the challenge of battles ahead. And it was through the cross that Christ died for our sins.

In all honesty, God intended for our lives to be lived this way from the start. Life on Earth is not forever. It is a stepping stone to eternal life in Heaven with Him. The only way out, the only way to eternal life in Heaven, is through—living day by day on Earth preparing for our new life to come.

I have been able to get through really tough times and over-come many fears, since I shifted this phrase to my advantage. Especially one of my biggest fears.

I suffer from a *gigantic* fear of needles.

Because of this, my necessary medical and wellness care has been put on hold for so long. I refuse to get blood work done or any other routine procedures that could ultimately help me if it means going within 10 feet of a needle. This phobia of mine makes me nervous even to go to the dentist, and since needles are not typically involved in dentistry, I realized I had a serious problem.

Luckily, I have been able to go a long time without ever having to be put in that position. I am up to date on all my immunizations and have been healthy enough to avoid any IVs or injections, that is, until 2021.

Finally, after more than a year of the coronavirus pandemic taking complete control of all our lives, the world was beginning to open up again, thanks to the development of the Covid-19 vaccines.

I had a big choice to make.

Considering how greatly Covid-19 had negatively impacted my life, you would think I would be jumping at anything that would set the world to rights and get me back on track. And I would have been, if I could get it into my body any other way than through a needle.

No matter how many times I repeated to myself that this vaccine could potentially save my life, I was still terrified of getting the shot. As time went by, I became one of the only people I knew who had not gotten the vaccine. I was starting to worry people would start clumping me in with the anti-vaxxers of the world, and I didn't want that reputation. *jokes*

The longer I waited, the more I made myself susceptible to a deadly virus and enabled fear to control my life. Seeing how tightly I was being gripped by this fear, I became aware of how much I was sabotaging my own wellbeing.

In the end, I got vaccinated, and I'm glad I did. After all, the only way out is through. Plus, I might have spared myself severe illness (or death, *yikes*) later down the line.

I truly believe the same concept applies to what you and I are going through right now.

You might be completely terrified to do something that will help you take the next step to move forward with your life. That is totally normal. It is *hard*, and it's hard knowing that it's going to be hard, if that makes sense. It's like we know that we will be ok someday, but we don't want to face the part in the middle. We don't want it to take time. We have gone through something unbelievably painful, and now we are rewarded with a journey filled with more pain, discomfort, and struggle. No wonder people need best friends to tell them to "get it over with." It seems like the most logical advice ever given, yet we still need to be reminded, because, if it were up to us, we would never start this journey of what we call *healing*.

The process is hard, but the decision to even want to start the process can be even harder. But if you weren't looking to start, you wouldn't have picked this book up. So now is the time to make the decision. Are you ready to walk forward? The only way out is through. There are no loopholes; trust me, I've tried very hard to find them.

Only you can walk your path through and out, but here is some advice from me that I learned on my own way.

Begin the journey: Make the decision for yourself. Do not let anyone pressure you into wanting to heal. It won't work. You can't do this anyone else's way but your own. Be fully content with the fact that you are willing to charge ahead and leave the rest all behind.

Believe in the journey: None of this would have any benefit to you if you are not willing to believe that better is out there, waiting for you to find it.

Take care of yourself on the journey: All the physical things need to happen. For starters, get back up, literally. I know there is a tear stain and a body shaped indent in your bed right now. Get yourself moving to take care of yourself. Reintroduce yourself to your brush, deodorant, and soap. But don't stop there. Continue to do those things for yourself that you need to do to feel and be your best.

Face forward in your journey: Keep your eyes fixed at the front at all times. There will be many times that the past will try to creep in and take you out of the journey to your future and your Plan B. Remain seeing the bigger picture so you are not easily swayed off course.

<u>Know that the journey never ends</u>: You're not on a journey to forget what happened or remove all trace of it from your life. That's impossible. Your journey is about becoming the person you are meant to be and finding the life that is meant for you. That's a process that has no ending, but it does have a beginning. *Now.*

This journey is here to stay, but it will most certainly not feel as difficult to walk through once you start progressing in it. I cannot wait for you to surprise yourself on how strong and determined you really are.

You probably don't feel that way right now, but I know you will. And you will get there by feeling all the other feels first.

It might be hard to believe, but all emotions need to be felt, especially the not so fun ones. Give yourself and your mind a safe space to feel some of the feelings you might have been putting off. I believe we do not allow ourselves to feel negative emotions because we feel they will do more harm than good, but I am here to advocate just the opposite. The truth is, when you don't allow yourself to feel those negative emotions, that's when they build up and cause a whole lot of damage to you and your life. You can't ignore them and hope they'll go away. The only way out of your negative feelings is through them.

It is important to feel. Feeling every inch of confusion, pain, sadness, betrayal, and loss is essential to helping you exercise those very valid feelings in an appropriate way, time, and place. When you're sad, let yourself understand why you are sad. When you are confused, allow yourself to explore why you are confused. When you are overwhelmed, give yourself space to slow down and unpick all burdens that are hovering over you. There are no bad emotions, and I think we tend to forget that. Hold onto the sad like you would hold onto the happy. Give that emotion time to express itself, for there is a reason you feel that way. That emotion is showing up for a reason, so allow yourself to sit with it until it decides to leave you. If you do not go through and process negative emotions, those feelings will check into the hotel in your mind, only to check out at a very, *very* wrong time.

That being said, I do think there is an emotion that should be held off for a while. A part of you needs to ensure that you do not get to this point until you are truly ready, for amazing things can happen when you feel it.

Anger.

CHAPTER 7

GET ANGRY

There are a lot of things in this world that get me heated, but rarely do I ever put that anger to good use. I more so break things, say a few foul words, and burn major bridges. And now you are probably wondering, how on Earth could this emotion be put into constructive, good use?

Anger is actually a secret weapon.

Has someone ever told you that you weren't capable of something? Maybe that you are second best and are falling short? How did you feel? Did you run away and cry hoping to never discuss it again? Did you tell other people hoping they take your side?

Or did it make you want to prove them wrong?

Anger should be packaged and sold right next to the energy drinks and pre-workout supplements, because if you use it in these moments, you will be unstoppable.

You and I have been told we don't measure up in some form or fashion. Our life is not how we built it up to be, and that is infuriating! So, by being able to channel our anger in a strategic way, we can start to shake in a world where someone else told us to stand.

Not only are we finding our Plan B, we are going to kick butt this time! Essentially, we are searching for a life that nothing and no one can destroy this time around. A life that even if it still doesn't turn out the way we hoped, it doesn't knock us off course.

No more blindsiding!

Have you come to the realization that this all is happening *for* you, rather than *to* you?

Me neither.

They say we will someday.

Is there something that you could be doing better? Maybe something you've always wanted to do, but never had the ability or time to do it? Now is the time. You are a blank sheet of paper.

Just imagine it.

You are your own diary. Your whole life is being jotted down while it is playing out. When things don't go as planned, you have to flip the pencil over and erase. The better the eraser, the less you'll be able to see what was there before.

Getting fired up in the gym brings good results, so why not get fired up in life?

This mentality reminds me of how I act every single time I take a spin class.

I am 30 minutes into the class, ready to fall off my bike, when the instructor shouts, "We are just getting started!" At that point, I am ready to unstrap myself from my seat and jolt to the exit door.

I always want to leave so much more than staying. I always think about what emergency I have to fake to publicly exit a very packed class just in case someone asks. And I always make sure to tell myself, at least 10 times, that I will never be taking a spin class in my life again.

But then it always hits me.

Am I willing to take the walk of shame out of this class, or do I stay and put as much effort as I possibly can into this workout for it to actually pay off? I mean, there really is no incentive for leaving class early. Sure, you get to breathe at a normal pace again, but losing weight and living a healthier, better life? Not going to happen if you quit.

I have no choice but to stay. The pros outweigh the cons every time, and all I know is the thought of me wanting to leave and knowing I can't, gets me *mad*.

The good kind of mad, where I get a rush of adrenaline pushing me through the last 30 minutes of the class because wanting to leave, everyone watching and judging you, and paying almost $60 for this kind of torture will surely get your blood moving in the best way possible.

So, get angry.

Let the feeling of wanting to escape get you through.

Let the feeling of people eyeing your every move get you through.

Let the feeling of others saying you aren't meant to succeed get you through.

Push through and take advantage of this type of stamina.

Once you feel anger in a productive way, you will know. If the anger you feel is producing thoughts of wanting to do some damage to the ones that damaged you, it might not be ready to go. And although it might seem productive to key cars and go all Carrie Underwood on some people, you will ultimately dig yourself into a deeper hole. Trust me on that one, folks. Like my mom always said, there is a one letter difference in the words anger and danger.

Anyway, let me get to the point.

What happens when an animal is backed into a corner? It attacks. Its primitive nature and will to live comes out.

Think of ways you could constructively "attack."

Protecting ourselves is key in finding our next paths. In this stage of rebuilding, we are now having to build more around us, to prevent outside invaders tearing us down again. By going into protection mode, you will be ready for any threat.

Now, when I say attack, I do not mean physically. This type of practice can and will only be mastered metaphorically.

So no payback, eye for an eye, vendetta, or anything of the sort.

I'm talking about a type of fighting back that will do much more than you could ever imagine.

"The best revenge is massive success." —Frank Sinatra

Success is our game plan.

The story of Joseph in the book of Genesis is an exemplary tale about how our greatness will ALWAYS be achieved through hardships and with Christ.

If you aren't familiar:

Joseph dreamt he was destined for something big. In a way where people would eventually bow down to him.

Whenever he had the chance, he always made sure people knew that. It wasn't until very soon, those people began to despise Joseph, made fun of him, and ultimately pushed him down a well.

Now, if someone were going around telling me how successful they would be, especially implying they would find more success than me, I would push them down a well too!

After some time had passed, Joseph's brothers, the ones who pushed him into the well, decided to sell Joseph to some passing by Ishmaelites, who would bring him to Egypt to work as a slave. During his time in Egypt, Joseph still decided to proclaim his dreams of greatness. After that, the pharaohs of Egypt decided to imprison him for getting on their nerves (The Tala Version).

One day, the King, who had been getting very mysterious dreams, needed some interpretation. He called on Joseph, releasing him from prison, and asked him to translate what these dreams meant.

Joseph told the King that his dreams are representing the status of the land. In seven years, they will have an abundance and *"great plenty in all the land."* However, the next seven years after that would leave the world in poverty, famine, and distress.

The King then struck up a plan to ensure they would be secure if and when that should happen.

The King asked Joseph to be in charge of the land's surplus of grains during the good years, to ensure they are prepared when the potential famine strikes. Once it does, people from all over the world will come to Joseph to collect food in exchange for something else.

One day, Joseph's brothers showed up begging for food from the surplus. As they were on their knees pleading to Joseph, they did not realize it was their brother standing before them. He then gave them their food and sent them on their way.

Although this story does go on, it just goes to show that true revenge is best served through honor and Christ.

I mean Joseph did tell his brothers that they would be someday bowing before him, and what do you know? They did!

Definitely familiarize yourself with the story if you want to know what the brothers did when they found out it was him! *Scandal!*

In this tale we learn several truths. These truths are essential to live by, and it primarily these reasons that the story of Joseph is one of my favorites.

1) Success doesn't happen overnight.

2) Through trust and perseverance with Christ, anything is possible.

3) Your success will always make the noise for you.

Keeping these things in your mind will make finding your next chapter much easier. You cannot find what you are looking for overnight. It takes time to build a new life, and learning to be patient and ok with that is pivotal.

Never for one second doubt your purpose. Allow God to reveal what that is for you. As of right now, the life you said goodbye to has been a clear indication that it is *not* your purpose. Learn to say goodbye to the ones who hurt you, for you are in a state of healing and revival. Lean on God as much as you possibly can. Especially when it feels like you have absolutely no one in your corner. When others doubt your greatness, just remember who holds the truth. Your *truth*, your *purpose*, your *greatness*, your *success*.

Stay silent in a world where there is constantly so much noise. Too many opinions, comments, angles, and advice have the ability to pollute your mind and convince you to think small.

Don't copy the behavior and customs of this world, but let God transform you into a new person by changing the way you think. Then you will learn to know God's will for you, which is good and pleasing and perfect. (Romans 12:2)

Imagine a world where all the ones who hurt you, doubted you, and secluded you end up seeing your name in lights, hearing your name on the TV, or seeing you on the front page! Let your success make the most noise. Let it shake the ground and shatter the ceiling. Find your purpose. If you don't know it yet...

Pray about it, and get angry.

CHAPTER 8

It's NOT Ok
to Be Ok

Humor me for a second.

You're in the hospital with internal bleeding. The only way to fix it is with surgery. You get nervous. You've never been under the knife before. You have never even stayed overnight in a hospital before. You are scared out of your mind.

The pre-operative team comes in and gets you ready for the procedure. Before they send you off, they ask you if you have any questions. You ask, "My surgeon, is he good?" They reply, "He's ok" and start wheeling you to the ER.

The End.

I don't know if it's my obsession with *Grey's Anatomy*, or

if I am taking this too literally, but the word "ok" has become pretty underwhelming to me.

Think about it. If you are someone who regularly gets professional opinions or reads online reviews, I am sure you want to hear words that are much more than "ok."

I say this because I have been all about challenging lately. Challenging the norms, and ways in which we operate, can lead to better outcomes than if we merely accept the status quo. As I observe people in my daily life, I am learning and understanding so much about how we interact with others and ourselves. It's amazing how much a person's body language can reveal about the state of their mental health. When I see someone who is clearly struggling, I always think to myself, Do they have a good support system in their lives?

Do you ever pass by cars on the roads and think, I wonder what that person's story is? What do they go through day to day? What trials and tribulations has the world put upon them? Do they have to deal with things like cancer, death, or abuse every day? I wonder all the time.

I am always thinking about other people's stories and what hardships they have to overcome each and every day.

I always wonder, are they living their best life? Or are they just "ok?"

When my whole world, life, goals, dreams, and plans got ripped away, I was probably being given some of the best advice in the whole world, the type of advice that would sound so poetic as soon as you heard it but hours later would be completely forgotten. What I do remember is the universal phrase that my advisers always ended with:

You will be ok.

Everything will be ok.

It is going to be ok.

Insert other variations. I'm sure you are familiar.

Every time, I wanted to shout, "No! Dang it! I don't want to be ok. I want to be more than that. I want to feel like Santa Claus...on Prozac...in Disney Land...getting laid!"

Shout out to Phoebe Buffay from *Friends* for that one!

Our (what felt like) best life was taken away, so how could someone expect us to be sufficient with just ok?

We are taking our life back, because we only get one. Why not make it more than ok?

Sure, there are many people who would agree that *ok* is a fine way of living. It isn't too much or too little. That works for some. Your life can be whatever you want it to be, and *you* get to decide what it is.

These days, if you ask someone how they are and they respond with, "I'm ok," you can assume they might not be having the best day. After all, someone that is having a great day would respond with words like "I'm well, good, great, etc..." Wouldn't you want to use words like that to describe your life rather than "ok"?

This isn't about achieving greatness but aspiring to have it. I don't want to put pressure on you about how and what you will do to acquire a great life, but I *want* you to at least want a great life.

Don't be the girl who can't get back on the horse. Let's face it—this will not be the last time things go wrong. Instead, be the *resilient* girl.

When I think of resilience, it helps me to remember that we are fighting through a life that has already been figured out long before we put on any armor. As Christians, our resilience shows our love and faith in God, because He has already created the path for us.

Resilience started to make sense to me when I started thinking about my life, start to end, what it would consist of. There is a reason we have to push forward—to fulfill His plans for us. There's no doubt that we as humans detour from God's plans for us every day, but in the end we must choose Him. Resilience isn't just about being strong or having thick skin. Also, being resilient does not mean you cannot feel pain. Resilience is all about how you allow your pain to not affect your future.

It can take some practice because resilience *is* a practice. You don't build resilience by going through one tough situation. It grows every time you bounce back from a challenge life throws at you.

And sometimes, girlfriend, when it rains, it pours.

Do you ever feel like a lightning rod for unfortunate events? Is it just me?

I don't know about you, but I would have thought that dealing with the destruction of one's entire life was enough for any person to deal with at a given time.

Apparently I was wrong!

As if losing my love, home, city, and stability wasn't enough, a few months into my healing and recovery, I was dealt more bumps in the road that I had to deal with on top of everything else.

I got laid off from my job, lost my best friend, and broke my foot. One thing after another kept happening, and it got to the point where I was constantly waiting for the next thing to go wrong, because it wouldn't be normal for things to actually go *right*. It also wasn't long before I was Googling "How do you know if you're cursed?"

But as these unfortunate events kept unfolding, something weird happened.

To my complete and total surprise, I was pushing through life much easier than I ever had. I wasn't getting derailed the way I would have before, and I was able to work through these things with a much clearer headspace. All the work I had been putting into becoming a stronger version of myself was starting to pay off.

You don't build resilience for just what you are going through right now; you are in a constant practice to keep the resilience going with you throughout your life.

It is almost like constantly working out and finally being able to lift a heavier weight that you would've never been able to lift if you weren't constantly exercising those muscles. With this in mind, you might think you know what resilience means, but allow me to break it down more.

Resist - Push away the urge to let things derail you.

Enforce - Be strict on yourself to not let yourself fall through the cracks.

Survive - This is survival of the fittest. Keep standing back up when you get knocked down.

Implement - Create strategies and coping mechanisms you can turn to when life gets too hard.

Laugh - Even when you want to cry, learn to find the humor in anything.

Immerse - Get out and do something. Keep yourself busy to stop your mind straying too far.

Embody - Transform your mind to incorporate a new way of thinking.

Navigate - Keep a clear mind to problem-solve without clouded thoughts or judgments.

Trust - Above all, keep trusting that every problem is all a part of a bigger plan.

Whether you saw it coming or you were completely blindsided, don't allow your current situation to knock you too far off course. There is so much more in store for you; you just have to keep wanting your great life.

I hope when people ask how you're doing now, instead of saying, "I'm ok," you respond with "I'm resilient."

CHAPTER 9

Unplug

Click! Ping! Swipe! Tag! Ring!

Hurry answer, like, comment, tag, post!!! The cyber world is waiting for all your glory and all the amazing things going on in your life right now!

But what do you post when there isn't really anything going on in your life? Even worse—if your life sucks?!

Social media can be the ultimate slap in the face in times like this.

Another engagement post, pregnancy announcement (planned or not, it still hurts either way), new job alert, or just a post about how someone really loves their life. Sounds like fun...for everyone else. After commenting "congratulations" a hundred times, it becomes to feel like torture.

Nowadays, when I express my praise and congratulatory wishes, I am doing so with major RBF behind the screen. #SorryNotSorry.

However, if none of this relates to you, then congrats on your amazing marriage, well-behaved kids, successful job, and superb 401k!

If this does resonate, then welcome to the club.

Social media is a great avenue for catching up with people whom you do not see regularly, recommending great vacation spots, and even influencing someone to buy something they might actually need. But when your whole world has come crashing down, you don't know what you are going to get hit with when you log in.

For a while, I kept getting worse and didn't understand how. Why has time passed, and I still felt the crippling waves of anxiety and depression? Shouldn't it have been getting easier as time went on?

I started to do some self-reflection to see what was inhibiting me from moving forward. I realized it was the thing I had been doing for most of my day— social media. Not just the checking it, but the overall temptation to post and the need to be certain it is the best photo of myself to post.

I then had to make the very grownup decision and unplug from the cyber world.

Don't get me wrong, it was not as freeing as it sounds. The anxiety of what I was missing, the messages I could possibly be getting, the sales I wasn't seeing, etc., kept me up at night for days.

Who knew I relied on other people's lives so much?!

But after that passed, and as time went on, I started to notice my dependency start to decline.

I guess social media was more than a dependency to me; it was an addiction.

According to a study, it takes a minimum of 18 days to break a habit. I knew I would need much longer.

Since I am an oversharing person, I posted my soon-to-be online hiatus on Instagram. I expressed it was not in my best interest for my mental health to be recovering while social media was still a daily activity for me. I needed to separate the two.

I received a huge outpouring of love and support. Before I logged off, I got message after message from people who were validating and understanding. It seemed that maybe I might have even encouraged others to follow my lead. But how come I never see that side of social media? We post all the good, but when was the last time you've seen the bad? When have you ever come across someone saying something that truly made you feel like you aren't alone in that way too?

Unplugging to me had multiple motives. I knew I would be finally able to hear my own voice without all the cyber noise, but I also knew I would have much more time on my hands, to be more constructive.

I checked my social media in the morning, waiting to order a coffee, working out, lying in bed, and even while driving (don't lie, you do it too). Now, I had an open calendar to do something else.

I had been given back all this time and knew there was only one thing I wanted to do with it.

Spend more time with **God.**

To spend time learning more about Him sounded amazing!

I didn't know what it meant or why I wanted to do that, it just came to me. It was almost like God had taken my distraction of social media away so that I could finally hear Him. It is what He has wanted from me for so long.

With this opportunity, I could speak with Him, learn from Him, study about Him, walk beside Him, and live through Him, all more than I ever could imagine.

Have you ever had a parent say something along the lines of "If only you knew your homework the way you memorized this song, you would have straight As."

The same idea applies here.

In all the time you would be spending on social media, being fully consumed by someone else's life, you could be growing your relationship stronger with God, being fully aware that the only person's life that matters is yours.

Imagine building a relationship that can and will never break for anything or anyone. You ever see people who have the strongest dependency on our Lord? The ones who never make a decision without speaking to God about it first? The people who learned how to slow down in life? That can be **you!**

Unplugging is the easiest way to do it. To go offline doesn't take any extra effort on your part. It isn't taking you away from any normal things you *have* to do on a day-to-day basis.

Now, I am not saying that you must learn everything about God in order to feel confident enough to return back to social media; however, I encourage you to do enough to challenge yourself.

I started to make a list so that this journey has more direction, for me and you.

1. Talk to God. Ask him for guidance in the morning, in the evening, and any spare moment you might have.

2. Don't just read the Bible; learn the stories! Learn them enough to where you feel confident enough to refer back to them at opportune times.

3. Utilize resources that will further your understanding about Him. Listen to worship music, podcasts, and sermons daily.

4. Keep materials around to remind you Whom you are constantly seeking. Change your background on your phone to a Bible verse or an inspiring quote. Keep Christ-centered visuals all around your bed, in your car, and at work.

Doing these things can ensure you make more room for Christ in your life.

Social media isn't the only thing that can steer us away from God, but it is something we can remove the easiest. Spending every waking moment with the Lord is essential. He can then reveal his true plans for us, without distractions and "comparisons" getting in the way. It is amazing how clear your vision can become once you turn off the screen.

Life is too short, so, in conclusion, would you rather spend more time living or posting about living? In limiting your screen time, you can also focus on yourself. You will have the ability to pay more attention to what your heart and soul crave the most. You not only fall deeply in love with God but with yourself too.

Taking one of the biggest distractions in my life away opened my eyes. We can learn so much about ourselves once we actually try. We all say we know ourselves well, but do we?

I recently found out that I am anemic. Before I found this out, I considered it to be normal to constantly be a pale, shifty, lightheaded girl with cold feet all the time. When things started to quiet down, due to less cyber noise, I started to notice things about my physical health that I normally wouldn't have taken the time to notice.

I was driving home one day after spending some time at the grocery store. On my way back, I felt a rush of nausea and sweat starting to drip down my forehead. I kept driving, hoping it would go away, but it never did. I was still 20 minutes from home and knew I wasn't going to make it. I immediately pulled over on a very busy highway and put down the windows to get some air. I started to dial my mother so that she could be with me while I was getting sicker and sicker. But the next thing that happened was not my mom answering the phone. It was me waking up face down on the steering wheel in a puddle of sweat. I had fainted on the side of the road.

I looked down at my hands, and I was still in the process of dialing my mother's number. The first 3 numbers had already been dialed, but I went out cold before I could finish. Even though I was still a bit disoriented from passing out, I wasn't surprised that this had happened. I had been lightheaded for months. After this, I immediately made a doctor's appointment to figure out what is going on.

Anemia is no joke, girlfriend!

If only I did something about these warning signs before it endangered my life and others' lives on the road. You have no idea how many important things are neglected just because of time being spent in front of a screen. Health and wellness, groceries, household chores, and our emotional health all get overlooked and put on the back burner.

Ever since that scary incident, I have been in tune with my

physical and mental health. I am constantly observing myself to reveal anything I might need to work on. Making sure my mental and physical health both remain in good condition, at all times, is routine now. It was never routine before. It is easy for us to neglect ourselves with life's constant perplexities.

Trust me, once you start taking care of yourself physically, your mental health isn't far behind either.

The relationships we have with ourselves and with God can fill the void we were previously trying to fill with the wrong things. Get ready to meet who you really are without all the filters! Fall in love with yourself without the constant pressure from profiles of people who seem to have it all figured out.

CHAPTER 10

Take the Trash Out

Since we are removing any and all things that can cause negative energy in our lives, I say we take it further than just the cyber world. It is time we clean house of physical the things that are prolonging our stress.

For me, that looked like many different things. I had a job that was giving me hell, a "best friend" who was treating me horribly, and a pile of old mementos reminding me of my pain that needed to be thrown away once and for all. It was clear that no matter how much work I put in internally, I would still be suffering due to the negativity surrounding me.

As much as we don't want to admit it, other people really do have an effect on us, and because of this, we must stay mindful about who exactly we are letting in. Most importantly, we need to focus on who needs to be kicked out. You might think that in a time of loss, saying goodbye to other people and things would not be possible, but I am here to prove just how beneficial it can be.

I had a best friend who was more like a sister to me than even my own sister. She and I were inseparable, and I valued our friendship more than any other one I ever had. As years went by, we experienced it all together—laughs, heartbreak, celebrations, mourning, successes, and failures. You would think that if either of our world's came crashing down that we each would be there to help pick up the pieces for one another. However, that was the exact opposite of what happened.

Since she was in my hometown, moving back home didn't seem all that scary. I knew I wasn't going to have to feel alone because she was just a short drive away. However, even though we were both so close, I never felt more far away from her. She became distant and detached from me and my situation, which ultimately left me feeling misunderstood and unwanted. It was hard to believe that through one of the hardest moments in my life, she was unreachable and very uncaring.

Unfortunately, due to the feeling of random rejection, I

became an even worse version of myself, in a time where I had been working very hard to calm down the ugly sides of me. I felt as if I was unwanted and uncared for, which led me to believe that all those things were true. All the hard work that had gotten me to finally stand on my two feet again came crashing down all over again. I became worse, which brought on more rejection and abandonment. Because of that, I started to solidify in my mind that these feelings were all I will ever know.

And just like that, my healing journey halted.

Shortly after being treated far from acceptable by my so-called best friend, my eyes started to open and see so many other people that have brought out the bad in me too.

Anyone that makes you feel unwanted, unloved, insecure, or a burden should never hold a place in your life. But believe it or not, there were many people who made me think less of myself that had been surrounding me for longer than they should have been allowed to. It wasn't until then that I started to realize an ugly truth.

There will always be people who don't have your best interest at heart. They will wish you ill and stab you in the back. They dread to see you succeed, and when you do, they will only stick around if your success benefits them. The ones that are so unhappy with themselves that his or her insecurities' project onto you to bring you down with them. The opportunists, the fakers, and the disingenuous reveal themselves every day; it just takes us to open our eyes and see it and act on it.

It was in that moment I knew I needed to say goodbye to someone I thought I would never say goodbye to. It was hard to succumb to that realization, for could I really afford to lose yet another important thing in my life? Even though there weren't good people in my life, was the toxicity still acting as some sort of filler for the silences and holes I felt all around me? Was holding onto the negatives just another way to keep me from feeling as lonely as I really was? I just couldn't fathom how removing all I maybe had left would bring me more peace. But somehow I knew that the feeling I had with these people could not possibly be any worse than the feeling of removing them from my life once and for all.

With that being said, I pulled out my mental magnifying glass to do some inspecting. Although I was ready to leave behind all the toxic people in my life, it turns out that people weren't just the problem.

I was working a job that was comparable to Alcatraz. I really wouldn't be able to give you just one reason that this job was especially heinous, for everyday it was something new. All I can say was is it was a mix of unfair pay, customer's cursing me out on a daily basis, an old boys' club hierarchy system, and so much more. Even with all the effort I put in to ensure my healing was on a good path, the second I clocked in every day, all the hard work had been erased. My mental health was already suffering, and unfortunately, this job was digging me into a deeper hole. I was suffering to the point that all the therapy, medication, and even prayers in the world were not getting through because of that wall of a job standing in my way.

It was time to stop fighting a battle I didn't need to fight anymore and leave my job.

Although I got laid off, it couldn't have come at a better time. I knew that never having to do another thing for that company would drastically change my life for the better. And because of that, I was surprisingly fine.

Now, I am not telling you this so that I can use this platform to bash my former friend or job. I am sharing that some of the most central things in our lives can be the ones that bring us down the most. In just a matter of one week, I lost a friend and a job, and due to how much toxicity they both brought into my life, I never felt better than when I released them. Even though I lost, I felt as if I gained.

Sometimes it takes going through something extremely hard to reveal who is there for you when you need them most, and, more telling, who is nowhere to be found. A friend that knows your tears just as much or even more than your smiles is a valuable person.

Because of this new revelation, a new layer of happiness had been revealed to me. Happiness isn't about just smiling all the time; it is about who has the power to wipe that smile off your face. We are now becoming protective of our well-being, and, unfortunately, there are many people and things that can prohibit your mental health staying up to the highest standard possible.

The million-dollar question in all of this is: Is there anything or anyone that might be holding you down?

In answering that question, you might need some help defining what that actually means.

To be held down, whether you are going through something traumatic or not, can look different depending on the person or source doing the holding. After all, sometimes the most harmful forces in our life are disguised as the most beneficial.

But I am not surprised! Even Satan disguised himself as an angel of light. (2 Corinthians 11:14).

People and jobs that make you feel unvalued and neglected are the first indicators that you should proceed with caution. For anyone to have that much of an effect on you shows just how necessary it is to do away with them. Now, don't go removing any and all things that might have upset you once or twice. Friends do fight and jobs do suck. I am speaking on the type of effect that is persistent. Reoccurring invalidation and disrespect to you and your mental health are what call for immediate dismissal.

When we don't break ties with the things that hold us down, bad things can happen. It might deepen the depression we are currently still battling, and, sometimes, it can make us lash out. I hate to admit that I have fallen into the trap of temper and rage. When it is all said and done, what could have been a clean break can undoubtedly turn into an explosive rampage towards the ones who have hurt us.

It is more important now more than ever to finally figure out who is helping your journey and who is hurting it. While having someone or something not right for you, you could be doing more damage to your mental health in a time that it should be the most protected. Figure this out sooner rather than later, for there is no time like the present to be surrounded by only the best this world has to offer.

If you feel as if you cannot afford to lose anything, check in and ask yourself, how much are they worth in comparison to your comfort, security, and success. In my life, once I said goodbye to two ultimately detrimental components of my life, I felt as if my vision became clearer. I was able to see without the constant fog of negativity that had been flooding my life for so long. I felt as if I could make more thought-out decisions and have better judgments. Ultimately, my healing accelerated faster than I could have ever imagined.

I like to think this feeling is comparable to the Mario Kart gaming world. Whenever you are on the track racing to the finish line, the game allows you to intentionally run into floating diamond-shaped crystals for extra headway in your race. Once you hit them, your car speeds up 10x faster, surpassing the other racers. That is what this type of acceleration felt like to me. All the time that I could have felt strong enough to find what is next in this journey, I was not going as fast as I could have been because of what was dragging me down.

Ever look around and feel as if someone else could have gone through your journey faster than you? That they would have been able to find his or her footing much easier? I think about this often, and whenever I do, I am reminded that these are the type of people who have become protective about who and what they let into their circle. These people preserve their own happiness, so if and when they get knocked off course, they are surrounded by quality people who pick them back up again.

In addition to kicking out the old, we need to replace them with this type of new: the type of people who value what we bring to the table; the type of people who validate and do not judge our emotions; the type of people who do not make you feel insecure; and, best of all, the type of people who only bring out the best in you and not the worst.

It is time to get in a Mario Kart state of mind, ready to accelerate to the finish line. Surpass all that has not been good for you and join the ones that have and can be at the end. It is time to do some house cleaning and ensure that the only people that are allowed in are the ones who care about your journey as much as you do. This might bring up some anxieties of having to find new companions and walk away from the ones you never thought you would leave behind. I am here to prove that losing the ugly is another way to gain the beautiful. Being happy in your surroundings, even with just one good friend, can feel like you are surrounded by a million good friends. It is time to get out of your comfort zone and make the hard decisions. After all, you don't want to go into your new, positive life bringing the negativity and toxicity with you.

So I ask you again: Is there anything or anyone holding you down?

CHAPTER 11

Baby, I Can Be
Your Motivation

It was my senior year of college, and, let's just say, I always thought senioritis was a myth. It most certainly is not. I was a few months away from the freedom of sleeping in as long as I wanted...

I mean, from being a well-rounded young adult, making my own choices in today's society.

wink, wink

I had all my classes in the bag and was taking very few hours, so not only was I going to graduate, I was going to commence with honors!

I was so close to walking across that stage, but there was one thing standing in my way: Economics 201.

One thing you should know about me is that I don't do math. I am the worst at math and any class that focuses solely on numbers. When under pressure, 2+2 will equal 11. So, basically chemistry, statistics, and personal finance are not my strong suits.

Must explain my bad spending habits.

Anyways, I was dreading it. I knew putting this course off for four years would eventually bite me in the butt. I traded my breezy senior year for long nights in the library, and spending over $100 on a calculator with more buttons than a seamstress.

However, I was determined. With a couple of easier classes, I could actually devote more attention to this course and surprise myself.

The first week was obviously very basic. Syllabus week, the difference between macroeconomics and microeconomics, etc...

As we had been working with the fundamentals for some time, we started learning a few mathematical formulas. And get this, it wasn't that hard! I was actually understanding the principles of basic Economics and knew that with just a few hours in the library, I would ace the first exam.

I remember it like it was yesterday. I studied all night reviewing every question on the study guide, and when the morning came, I felt prepared. It was memorable because it was the first time I felt prepared for a math-oriented test, *like ever.*

Have you ever taken a test where you knew every answer? You even see the answer in your head before picking it out of the multiple choice? That was me.

A few days went by, and I knew we would be receiving our results any time. I checked the online portal constantly, and it was honestly such a good feeling. I could already see a good grade in my head before on paper.

And there it was—F. (No, I am not cursing, that is what I got. Although now that I am thinking about it, it could also be a very appropriate reaction to how I felt in that moment. So yeah, I am cursing too.)

I was devasted. I don't know what went wrong, or how I could have done so poorly.

I literally went through the five stages of grief because of that grade, and for a week I swore that my test was mistakenly switched with someone else's. Switched at birth, y'all!

I felt defeated, and considering it was still so early in the semester, the feeling of failure crept up way sooner than expected. It was only the second week of the semester, and I was having the hardest time paying attention in that class. I felt like it was pointless to be the slightest bit interested. Any information that I retained, whether I knew it or not, would still end up in a bad grade. I soon started showing up late, and it wasn't long before I stopped showing up at all.

And, to be honest, this class wasn't an easy one to skip. It wasn't first thing in the morning and not at the end of the day. It was smack dab in the middle of my other classes. In order to skip, I would still have to stay on campus and kill time every day. Plus, the obvious reason of failing the class all together would inhibit me from graduating college in the end. But I still stopped going. That must have been where the senioritis kicked in, because for some reason I thought I was invincible and would magically pass this class without having to attend ever again.

Needless to say, I never graduated from college.
Sorry to all that came to my graduation party.

I was still able to walk at graduation due to me only having one credit left, however. I would say that basically makes me a college graduate, right? Ugh.

Even though I am currently working on finishing my degree, I think about this story often. It was and still is a reminder that with self-doubt and discouragement nothing can be achieved.

It reminds me of how other things in my life haven't played

out the way they should have, too. After all, isn't that why we are here? Things have not played out the way they *should* have, or at least the way we *thought* they should have.

There was something missing in my Econ class, and it was the very thing missing when healing through my own downfall. Lack of motivation.

Motivation is the will to keep going, and self-discipline is what you need when the journey hits unexpected bumps along the way, like the constant reminders of your loss that keep popping out of the woodwork. Triggers are everywhere, making it even harder to move forward when we are constantly confronted with all that we are trying to forget.

A museum of remnants and memories seems to follow me wherever I go. In most cases, memories are beloved treasures. Memories have a safe place in our mind to bring back the things in life we can't hold onto forever. They are stored like old home movies, and when we need little pick-me-ups or a random burst of laughter, we pull them out. But not all memories give us the same warmth and comfort.

So how do we continue on without letting every little sight, smell, song, taste, sign, saying, and whatever else not derail us?

When I originally moved back in with my parents, I felt like a guest. My childhood bedroom didn't even feel like the one I lived in for 22 years. When I moved out, I took basically everything I had. And since my mom and dad never did the "normal" thing and turn my room into a gym, it was a space filled with old, sad furniture with no other place to go.

It was tough to be there, and I am not going to lie about that. Every time I woke up and even when I went to bed, I kept having the same recurring thought:

"I cannot remember the last time I woke up alone."

"I cannot remember the last time I went to bed alone."

Even though the last time was literally the day before, I still got those thoughts every morning I woke up. And that was the problem. Every single morning, I woke up and got my day off to a negative start, reminding me of my current status, as if I I was going to forget anytime soon. I knew that I needed to kick those thoughts out of my head for good. But was that possible? How do we erase memories that our brain involuntarily stores, whether we want it to or not?

We can't.

Unless you suffer from amnesia or major alcoholism, we are designed to store an infinite amount of information in our brain. So how do we conjure up the world's strongest self-discipline to not allow these things to make us officially throw in the towel?

I don't know if you are like me, but I go through a whole day being constantly bombarded with memories, and most of the time, they are unwanted. I come across so many objects that hold sentimental value that I just can't seem to let the worth attached to it go.

Because my past life tragically ended while I was in the middle of building my dream home, I cannot even pass by houses under construction without having all the feels. I legit have a phobia of construction paper now.

Even though that is the most extreme case, I still can attach a sentiment to any inanimate object. And I am sure you have too.

"Oh my gosh, he loved Mozzarella sticks" *queue cries*

"I bought this dress to impress him." *queue cries*

"We passed by this road once." *queue cries*

"That was the exact same cabinet I picked out for our kitchen." *queue cries*

I could go on forever!

But you get the point.

Consequently, getting back up and living life again almost feels like a trap. Reminders are constantly everywhere, and if you are in a fragile, sensitive state, it can be exhausting. You are not only warding off unwanted thoughts in your mind but are now living in fear of the triggers you might also be faced with. How can we even think about self-discipline when we are this exhausted? I settled on believing that would be an impossible task for me. If I didn't even have the energy to brush my teeth, I surely was not equipped to keep my sanity together when faced with some of the biggest triggers in my life.

Because of that, I stopped leaving the house for good. I just couldn't take that many chances of getting completely grief-stricken in public anymore. Staying in felt like the safest place I could be during this time, which is especially true since we were still in the middle of a global pandemic. Eventually, I would exhaust all tears with reminders in my house until it didn't bother me any longer. And even that brought on a type of peace that thought I would never experience again.

Several months had passed of me doing this. Food was constantly being delivered, Netflix was always on, and my bed was a couple feet away at all times. And although it was peaceful, my extrovert nature started to kick in. I hate sitting around and cannot stay in the same place for too long. I thrive off of people and stimulations. It wasn't long before I started to get more cabin fever than the dude in *The Shining*. But was I ready to attempt the outside world again? I may have not been ready to do anything big like date or go to a party, but could I stomach just leaving the house again?

I didn't know how and what I could do to feel the most comfortable. I needed a little push, but I didn't know what that push would be.

I started to realize that I needed to do some inside changes to prepare myself for bigger changes on the outside.

I quickly knew just the thing!

Every morning I woke up and reminded myself I am in a place I never imagined myself being in, surrounded by things such as dusty, old furniture and bad memories. If it weren't for me reminding myself, the rattle noise coming from my old bed certainly would do it. Every morning, I was being prompted by all the old, and it made losing what I lost all the harder. With that, I decided to rewrite that room's story.

I was in full home improvement mode, changing everything. I changed the paint, furniture, lighting, and even the doors! I needed to start waking up in a place that finally felt like my own again.

I am not going to lie; it was still challenging. Although this was a great step into a new and beautiful direction, I still was being confronted by unwanted thoughts.

This is a great color, and it is going to look so good when it's done, but I still never imagined my life would be like this. I thought the next time I would be painting walls would be in the new home we built.

And when I had these thoughts, I had to take a few breaks and get my mind back on course. On one of these breaks, I started to realize something I wished I found out earlier. These thoughts were never really going to disappear from my brain. The only thing that was going to change was my determination not to let them knock me down every time. It was the motivation that had been missing all along. My sensitivity wasn't the problem; it was my motivation that needed some work. The self-discipline didn't get easier, but I, for once, had some direction, and sometimes just a small game plan is all you need.

I grabbed the paint brush and started to paint over what had been there before, literally, and metaphorically.

It felt so good to actually see what possibilities might lie ahead. In a world where I couldn't see the other side, and never thought I would again, it was the most magical feeling I ever had.

That being said, don't beat yourself if you're not feeling motivated now, if you can't see the possibilities yet. The hardest part about getting back up on the horse is not that we don't want to put in the work, but that we're afraid to fall back off. You are in an incredibly vulnerable state, and it can take the slightest misstep to push you over the edge.

Plus, if the reminders are too unbearable for you to even function, it's possible there's something else you could be combatting—PTSD.

When we think of PTSD we tend to think about war veterans and plane crash survivors, but it doesn't take horrific and near-death experiences for someone to suffer from PTSD. It can appear when we go through a variety of conflicts and traumas in life, within family, relationships, work, or health.

Studies show that the defining symptoms of PTSD include unwanted flashbacks, intrusive thoughts, distress from literal or symbolic reminders, becoming easily upset or feeling on edge, and many more.

I identified with pretty much each one. Did you? They say everyone will go through at least one traumatic event in his or her life, and what you and I have gone through certainly constitutes that.

PTSD can inhibit us from going on with our lives because the make-up of our brains has been drastically altered. We are doubtful of others as well as ourselves, we avoid many places that could spark an unwanted memory, and we even feel unsafe in our own skin.

It is no surprise that many people have difficulty moving past a terrible situation that has occurred in their life. When we go through trauma, our mind starts to create a new pattern for us. Our brains start to believe that our environment is danger-ous and that we should be guarded, untrusting, and pessimistic. We can become scared to be happy because unhappiness has proven to not be too far behind. Being unhappy has become familiar and comfortable, so we cling to it. That is what trauma does. It rewires your whole personality.

I believe we struggle to move beyond trauma because we know it will unexpectedly show up in our future in one way or another. Triggers are inevitable, so why would I do all the hard work to put the past behind me when it will undoubtedly show up again anyway? The disheartening fact is that we will never be able to get rid of trauma in this world, but we can change how it affects us. We aren't saying "no" to trauma; we are saying "yes" to motivation. We cannot undo a mental illness, but we can alleviate its impact on our lives. I recommended therapy earlier in this book, and I'll say it again here. Especially if you think you may have PTSD, try therapy! It may not be fun, but you know what's really not fun? Living at the mercy of PTSD.

I mention PTSD to show that you are not combatting something small. It needs to be celebrated that you have decided to push through. Celebrate the power of pushing through a circumstance that has taken the faith, power, and unfortunately, the lives of so many.

❧

*Look straight ahead and fix
your eyes on what lies before you
(Proverbs 4:25)*

If only I'd known better than to give up so easily in my Economics class, I could've saved myself a lot of time, money, and self-inflicted damage to my mental health and self-esteem.

Sometimes we are our biggest critics. Other people do not have nearly as much power to incapacitate us as our minds do. Sometimes you have to stop listening when your mind tells you that it is impossible to move on. **Rely on me to be your motivation, girl!** You will never succeed if you don't try, so don't let your mind deceive you that you can't move past this loss to achieve a bright, beautiful future! What you've been through does not have to determine who you will become and what you will do.

And in case you didn't know, you don't need a college degree to write a book.

CHAPTER 12

Derailing

You may have recently found out that grief doesn't really come in the "so called" five stages.

If you are anything like me, it has gone something like this: denial, anger, denial, anger, denial, anger, bargaining, depression, acceptance, depression, depression, depression, bargaining, acceptance, denial....and it just keeps repeating.

Emotions are running high. You might be experiencing the highest of highs only to drop to the lowest of lows in a matter of seconds. We are in a push/pull kind of mindset. We are charging through a pain that seems scary to leave behind. It's agony. Our minds are tortured so staying positive doesn't come as natural to us anymore. It's like we have Stockholm syndrome towards our own hurting. We feel comfortable in our suffering minds because "it can't get any worse," and somehow that can be calming.

However, since time does heal and *whatever*, it can become much easier to let that kind of morbid comfort go as time goes on.

About eight months in after my world came crashing down, I was doing better than I ever thought I would be able to do again. With much support and a whole lot of prayer, I was starting to see the other side of the darkness. I was eating regularly, making decisions, and, even the most basic thing, smiling again. I hate to admit it, but *they* were right. The ones who said I would be able to smile again. The ones who said I would start to forget about the plans I had before. The ones who said I would ultimately believe in this thing we call *life* again.

It felt amazing to finally go to bed and wake up with a feeling of liberation and peace, instead of anxiety and worry. The days were becoming much easier to get through, and the nights were finally not being interrupted by nightmares and racing thoughts. I was finally on the path that would lead me out of the darkness for good.

This wave of peace and calmness lasted for weeks, when for

me to remain in that state for longer than two days was a huge accomplishment in itself. I had been in such a high state for so long that I was convinced my healing was nearing the end. I was ready to throw away my meds and even cancel all remaining sessions with my therapist. Not only was I feeling happy, but I believed in why I was. Things were starting to look up in my life. I onboarded with my dream job, I was making new and quality friends, I was losing weight, and pretty much everything was coming up Tala.

I felt healed!

I could tell that my friends and family also noticed a difference in my mood. Everyone kept telling me how proud they were of my strength and persistence to see the light. For the first time in months, I came up for a breath of fresh air. I was no longer drowning in a pool of confusion and distress.

Then suddenly, BAM! I was knocked off course. I fell off the rails of the positive streak I had been on. In other words, I *derailed*.

One minute I was hustling through life, pushing through any and all adversity that could pop out at me, and the next minute I fell into a deep depression that hindered me from even functioning at all.

Out of what felt like nowhere, I was plunged into weeks of living in a discordant mind.

10:00am: refreshed and hopeful

12:00pm: anxious, on edge

3:00pm: exhausted and drained

5:00pm: confident and powerful

5:01pm: suicidal

7:00pm: optimistic and assured

9:00pm: trusting and patient

Repeat the next day.

Getting knocked off course during this type of journey is scary. Something that derailing is notoriously good at doing is convincing us that we have ruined our healing. We feel like we are back at square one. When we experience this, we get angry at ourselves and believe we have completely erased all of the previous work we put into our journey. Derailing can make us feel ashamed that we aren't going in the straight line we expected to go in. Instead, it's a lot of back and forth, up and down, and stop and go. It is like driving cross-country and pulling over every two minutes, making an already long journey even longer.

But like it or not, derailing is part of the process, and it's actually a sign that things are going well.

You couldn't be thrown off track if you weren't on the tracks to begin with. This is where that resilience we spoke about earlier needs to be executed. Resilience will catch your derailing before it can stick around for too long. Derailing is like an in-law that always overstays their welcome. If you make them too comfortable and allow them to freely roam as they please, they will never leave. However, if you make it known you cannot host them for too long due to prior commitments, you can deal with them, knowing they will leave soon. In this case, your prior commitment is your journey and healing, and it cannot afford to be put on hold for your "derailing in-laws."

Just know that derailing is natural and, actually, *necessary* to get you to the other side in your journey.

Derailing is like a downpour on a day you'd planned to spend having an outdoor adventure. You wake up expecting to have a great day, only to find yourself stuck inside staring at the rain. Although your outlook might be bleak, it doesn't mean you will feel this way for the rest of your life. Rain goes away, and derailment is temporary. It is important to keep that at the forefront of your mind. Much like anything that is unpleasant, this too shall pass. Just like when you have horrible menstrual cramps, you have to take care of yourself and wait it out. Derailing is a waiting game, and although that doesn't sound very hopeful and promising it is all you can do without doing permanent damage.

The reason I wanted to talk about derailing is to help you normalize it. I am sure you have fallen off the wagon once or twice so far, and you feel as if you are helpless when it happens. Ironically, you are doing everything right. Just remember to not beat yourself up when you get derailed.

It took me realizing that grief isn't linear, and to stop giving myself a hard time each time I "took a step backwards." I believed that when you went through something, you grieved it and got over it. That is, until I actually experienced grief myself and learned that grief does not work like that, *like*, at all.

So, if you feel like you've taken a step backwards, I'm here to tell you that you are not moving backwards. You are simply standing still. You are standing firm, not allowing yourself to drastically reverse or try to speed up. Some people hate the feeling of derailment so much that they try to jump over the finish line so they don't have to feel their feels. I hate to break it to them, but that is just a recipe for more derailment in their future. You might not feel graceful right now, but you are in a stable place, riding out the storm. You are waiting for it to pass while still holding onto all the knowledge and progress you acquired leading up to this. Don't move forward. Don't go backwards. Just stand still.

Let the derailment happen. Learn from it. It can unveil more about your healing than you may have ever known. Let your loudest emotions be revealed and explore them.

You can be both strong and weak.

You can be both resilient and still need a break.

You can be both independent and still need others.

Derailment is not a bad thing. It is your journey. If you derail, it must mean that you were soaring for quite sometime.

After all, what goes up, does come down eventually.

CHAPTER 13

Feeling Gratitude

I was at dinner the other day with one of my old friends, Lauren.

She is the kind of friend that will probably never pick up this book. I mean, why would she need it? She is the blonde bombshell you hate to love and love to hate. The kind of girl that knows she's pretty, but not enough to make her self-absorbed. She's skinny, but also thick in just the right places. She got married to her high school sweetheart, lives in a gorgeous home, and racks up a very nice paycheck every week. So, I doubt this book will ever make it onto her coffee table.

This particular dinner was one of my first times out in several months. It had become too hard to see people with my newfound social anxiety, but something about Lauren and sushi always brightens up my mood. So, I agreed to go.

While she looked fabulous in her white low-cut bodysuit, showing off that awesome boob job, I was sitting in three-day-old sweats with no makeup and a messy bun on the top of my head. I dressed the way I felt for sure.

Since we hadn't seen each other in almost two years, I took her through my life. As I went through the motions of telling her how my life has landed me here, she abruptly stopped me.

She seemed so annoyed and needed to tell me why.

"Do you see this?" she asked.

As I stopped my story and looked down, she was drawing attention to her nails.

After telling me how she had just gotten her nails done that day, she proceeded to tell me something about them.

She started pointing to these tiny, black polish residue specks the nail technician left on her nails. When I say tiny, I mean get a microscope that detects viruses from a lab kind of tiny.

So here I was, with my life spinning out of control, and there was Lauren, whose only afflictions came from a bad day at the nail spa.

It reminded me that we all know a Lauren.

If you ask me, I would much rather have tiny little black

specks on my nails than go through what I was currently experiencing. I bet you can remember instances where you were ready to trade hardships with someone else.

2020 was the year to share those hardships with the rest of the world. Weddings, much needed vacations, and more—all canceled. Whether big or small, we ALL can remember something that didn't go according to plan that year.

However, I was still ready to trade anything else for what I was enduring.

A wedding being cancelled didn't nearly sound as bad as an entire life being called off. Yes, from a financial and emotional standpoint, it can be extremely tough, but at least those couples were still together and going in some direction. At least, they would eventually get married. At least those women had thousands of other brides in the same boat as them. At least venues can offer them a new date once it is safe to have a wedding.

At least.

At least.

At least.

When life doesn't go as planned, it is almost unimaginable to feel the "at leasts" for yourself the way you would for others.

"Oh Tala, at least you didn't marry the guy and have kids

with him."

Every time someone said that to me, I tried to think of a million reasons why, even without those things happening, mine is still the worst situation anyone could ever find themselves in, ever.

Because I knew somewhere out there, someone was telling another young woman like me, *"At least you weren't living together,"* or *"At least you weren't building a home together."*

I couldn't help but think about how someone else's "at leasts" were my reality.

After all, if a woman does in fact end up marrying a terrible man and having kids with him, what would her "at leasts" be then?

The other day my friend Zac and I were discussing our luck with dating apps. We had been swapping stories and venting about our pet peeves with the opposite sex on these sites. Things such as chewing with their mouth open, jealousy, and being too clingy all came up.

He told me about this one instance that I believe we all have experienced. He and a girl he met online were getting involved in an act that is considered to be the most flirtatious thing you can do in this day and age. He would like a bunch of her pictures on social media, waiting for her to reciprocate. Once she would, he would do it again. And so on, and so forth. This can go on for weeks, and it did. He told me that it was his time to finally slide into those DMs to take the flirting to the next level. They had been messaging for a couple weeks about all the normal things—jobs, weather, etc... So, he felt it was time to ask her out on a date.

After he did, he noticed she had seen the message and was anticipating a response soon.

But it never came.

She never responded and Zac was completely annoyed. As he was telling me what happened, or better saying what didn't happen, he ended it with this.

"I mean, she could have at least told me no."

When he said that, I thought of how I would feel if someone ever did that to me. When I'd asked guys out, I'd always gotten a response back, either the good ole "I'm not looking for a relationship," "I'm busy," or even "I have a girlfriend."

And every time I received a response like that, I would say to myself, "At least just don't respond to me."

I realized something very pivotal then: We will never be happy with any type of response that isn't exactly the one we want. Whether they would message me back or not, I would find every way possible not to be happy with the outcome. We always want what we can't have, and end up always unhappy with what the cards have dealt us in these instances. We tell ourselves that we would be much happier if someone has given us the complete opposite treatment than they have given. If they message me back, I would think, "At least just don't respond." And if they don't respond, I would think, "At least just message me back."

I needed to find a way to change my thinking to allow myself to be happy with any circumstance life hands me. No matter what someone says or does, I wanted to instill a pattern of appreciation with every end result.

This all got me thinking about the word we should use every day but only end up using once a year—thankful.

Whatever is good and perfect is a gift coming down to us from God, our Father, who created all lights in the heavens (James 1:17)

What are we actually grateful for in this world, and is it just the good days? For us to be grateful for everything in life is God's intentions, but it rarely goes like that. Being grateful for just the good days inhibits us from keeping the momentum going on the bad ones. After all, no one needs an extra push on the easy days. Having gratitude on both the good and bad days allows us to enjoy our life much more.

By practicing the art of gratitude, you will be able to stub your toe with a smile still on your face, in no time.

Now's the time when I talk about that wonderful (annoying) saying, "Everything happens for a reason."

I believe that saying is actually very beautiful despite it being the most cliché thing I have ever written before. "Everything happens for a reason" only makes sense when that reason is finally revealed. And since that saying is one of the most wildly popular mantras in the world, the reason must exist.

I started to reflect on my own life to pull from times I had seen this wisdom actually play out. In coming to terms with all of our pain, pulling from our own life experiences is sometimes the only thing that can provide us a guarantee that moving forward is for the best. However, this was not the case for me, not at first. Losing my Plan A was the worst thing that had ever happened to me, and I really didn't see any reason for it to have happened.

I needed something, anything, that would allow me to stop

thinking everything in my life was just as bad as it seemed. I needed a story that gave me some sort of hope in moving forward. What have other people gone through? With a world with more than 7 billion people in it, there are bound to be some pretty wild stories. What twists of fate have allowed others to look on the "bright side?" I wanted to see a success story that could have easily taken a very wrong turn on its journey, a story where someone can point to a time that a change of plans in their life had ultimately saved them, a time where someone could prove *that this amazing thing* wouldn't have happened, if *that horrible thing* didn't happen.

In search of this story, I found myself thinking about the worst day for my country in my lifetime: September 11th, 2001. On a day like that, what were the "at leasts?"

I did some research and came across a woman named Crystal Tatum.

Crystal had been engaged and soon would be relocating with her fiancé to New York City for work. She had accepted a job working in the second tower. Very soon before the wedding date, she found out her fiancé had been cheating on her. Crystal called off her wedding and canceled her move. With the events that played out on 9/11, Crystal dodged more than one bullet that day.

This was her Instagram caption a couple years ago on the 9/11 anniversary:

"I remember being so excited about moving to New York and getting a job in World Trade Center 2 as a financial broker. Then my heart got broken and I didn't move. As I watched the events unfold on September 11th, I was literally shaking thinking that could have been me. That would have been me if I had forgiven a cheater. We never know why things play out the way they do so I encourage you to do what feels right in the moment. To those lost on this day, an entire nation remembers and honors you."

After I read her story, I decided to find out more about her life now. I had to know what her Plan B consisted of. She went on to live in Texas, becoming the CEO of her very own communications firm and enjoying a pretty adventurous life, according to her very lively Instagram feed. But also I came across something else. She was diagnosed with breast cancer. When I saw that, I immediately felt let down. I needed a story that was going to help me find my inner gratitude. I needed a fairytale ending I could bet on. But when I found out she had been sick, I felt like I was going to be sick myself. How could I have faith that everything happens for a reason when Crystal's life looks like one tragic event after another? Where was the guarantee that if I choose to finally be thankful for the events that took place, that something even worse wasn't just waiting for me around the corner? I guess in all of this I forgot where I am.

I am on Earth, the flawed planet with sin, glitches, devastation, and let downs. Tragedies and hardships are never going to go away. In fact, the only guarantee is that our time on Earth will be full of trials.

Life doesn't promise us one hardship, and I feel like we purposely try to forget that. We'd like to think that once you go through something tough, you aren't due for anymore unlucky or dreadful circumstances. I needed that wake-up call.

But it still haunted me. Why had Crystal been put through such a difficult time, only to survive and struggle even worse later? Then suddenly I got this thought, as if God had said it to my face.

He said to me: *I saved her life, so that she would have the chance to fight for her life.*

When that thought came to me, it changed me for the better. It gave me a deeper understanding of life and the tests within it.

I tried to put myself in her shoes and wondered which life

I would've chosen: Plan A—getting married (to a cheater) and starting the dream job only to die in the office—or Plan B—getting diagnosed with breast cancer but still having a fighting chance to live. I would choose life. No matter what that life looked life, I would choose it. I imagine Crystal's "at leasts" would go something like this:

At least I am still here.

At least my life is still mine to fight for.

And for that, I am grateful.

That's when I realized that the feeling of losing everything wasn't *actually* losing everything. Yes, my life looked completely different overnight, but when the tornado finally cleared, I still had a life. I still had a place I could sleep safe and sound at night, with food in my stomach, with my family and friends to love me, and much more! Not everyone is so fortunate.

I don't believe we lose sight of gratitude for what we have because we don't want what we have; it is simply that we get consumed by our disappointment over what we've lost. And that's to be expected, for a time. But it's important to realize, after the storm has passed, that you're still here. What you have to do now is take stock of what you have and find gratitude for it. The building blocks for your Plan B are already in your life. Gratitude will help you find them and start building again.

p.s. Crystal is cancer free!

CHAPTER 14

Manifest It

We were all taught in school that our physical actions are made of energy. Now, many scientists and psychologists say that our thoughts and emotions are also made up of that same energy. Just like a body in motion stays in motion, a mind that focuses on the positive or the negative will continue to see the positive or the negative.

This is the power behind The Law of Attraction or Manifesting. You have the ability to create a positive life for yourself with just your thoughts.

We have all experienced The Law of Attraction in our lives, whether we were trying to or not.

Have you ever thought about a specific TV show episode

before, and then, later that week, seen it on rerun?

That, my friends, is you experiencing the Law of Attraction.

I once dated a boy named Fox in high school. He was my first love, and a great one to be honest. Me being the overly dramatic person that I am, as you can imagine, the breakup was the end of the world for me. The day after we broke up, I had been driving around trying to take my mind off of him. On my drive I saw anything you could put the word "Fox" onto. Billboards, buildings, businesses, products, etc...

Fox Den Country Club, Fox WTNZ-Fox43, Fox Road, Fox & Farmer Attorneys at Law, and SO MUCH MORE!

That was all in one trip, and it seriously sucked!

Years later, I realized it definitely didn't have anything to do with Knoxvillians being obsessed with the name Fox. It had to do with what my mind was honing in on. Me focusing on that word allowed my eyes to notice it more than I ever did before. Those signs had always been there; it was my thoughts that had changed, which allowed me to view them differently for the very first time.

If you can relate, you are practicing the Law of Attraction and Manifestation without even trying.

Now, I'm not going into the nitty gritty details. There are

plenty of other books on that. I am simply advocating this technique to encourage you to envision a better life. Your mind may be cluttered with negative thoughts right now, which are preventing you from attracting what is best for you.

So what I want you to do is to think of your *happy place*.

You read me right. What is your happy place?

Mine has been the same for years, and before I share it with you, just know it is lame.

Any time I feel anxious, upset, or even bored on a long car ride, I envision the place in my mind that brings me comfort, serenity, and peace.

I escape in my mind to my parent's living room, eating hibachi, and watching *Friends*. That's it.

I told you it was lame.

It is my favorite place, favorite food, and favorite show. The simplicity of it brings me so much joy every time.

I know it is not what the cliché happy places usually look like. It is not rolling around in dandelions on a meadow, but it works for me.

Once you're in yours, notice how it makes you feel. Do you feel the tension in your body relax and the worries in your mind calm down? When you open your eyes, does the world around you feel a little bit better? That's pretty powerful.

Now imagine the power of envisioning your *happy future*.

I am sure the loss of your Plan A has got you thinking, "What's next?" And in all of that thinking, I bet you've imagined it. Now I'm asking you to imagine it so vividly that all you can see is what's to come rather than the past. If you lost a job, imagine a new and better one, maybe even one where you're the boss. If you lost a love, imagine the person who will come into your life and make this all worth it.

You *could* be predicting your whole life moving forward without even lifting a finger.

I recently came across this guy online whose profile took my breath away. He was a Christian, teacher, basketball coach, and very easy on the eyes. I think I fell in love. I thought of how amazing it would be to have a shot with a guy like that.

I soon started envisioning being with this man. Dating, marriage, kids, the whole story. I even would play out day-to-day scenes in my head of what life would look like.

Yes, I know, this does sound somewhat crazy, but it has had multiple, amazing results.

For one thing, anytime I ever missed my past or the life I

had lost, I thought about this new one in my head. I thought about how this new man is more what I want than what I would have had. By imagining my future Christ-following husband and father to my children, I felt relief and hope!

It's like, you might have crashed your Honda, but you're saving up for a Ferrari. You allow your mind to dream bigger and better.

In visualizing this better life, you can turn it into a reality.

Now I am not saying I will magically end up with the hunky basketball coach, but I am allowing myself to attract people who are good for me into my life. And I know, one day, I will get the happily ever after that is *meant for me*.

You cannot begin to start life over if you don't actually believe in it. You don't necessarily have to believe in manifestation, but you do need to believe in the underlying themes of manifestation, which are to have faith and be positive.

It is important that when using the power of visualization that you are doing so purely with optimism. Visualizing the many amazing things you wish to have in life is practicing hope. It allows you to gain confidence as you acclimate back into the world. By transforming your mind into a positive place, visualizing positive outcomes, you can give yourself back the hope you lost with Plan A.

Let me share a little story with you about how I transformed from a skeptic into a *manifestor.*

There is one place every fashionista wants to go at least once in his or her life:

New York Fashion Week!

This week is full of top models and hot runways showing off today and tomorrow's next fashion trends! It is a place where all the normal people, like us, get to go to some of the fashion industries' biggest events. Being obsessed with all things fashion and beauty, NYFW has always been on my bucket list, and the opportunity finally came!

A couple years ago, NYFW fell right on my birthday, which made it the perfect excuse to pack up and head to the Big Apple. Through my own fashion blog, I had a few connections to get me into all the right places and would be able to experience NYFW the way it was meant to be.

I called my best friend up and told her we were going to New York City!

Very quickly into our planning, we learned that New York City ain't cheap, and my dreams were starting to get squashed. Unless we were willing to stay at a dingy motel that was hours away from the city and find a roundtrip flight for $30, we were not going.

In all my disappointment and uncertainty, my best friend somehow stayed hopeful. She is the ultimate expert when it comes to attracting the best life has to offer. As we were doing our research, she kept saying things like, "Everything that is meant to be will happen for us."

As a couple weeks passed and I went on with my sad, pathetic, not NYFW life, I saw that dream drift further and further away. It seemed as if I was not going to go.

Then I had received an email inquiry that changed the way I lived forever.

Hi Tala -

My Knoxville-based marketing/advertising/pr firm has represented McGhee Tyson Airport in Knoxville for the past seven years. We are currently working on a promotion for new American Airlines service to NYC (LaGuardia). This is a joint promo between TYS and American Airlines.

We have been looking at social media influencers in both the Knoxville and New York City markets (we wanted someone with ties to both cities). If you are interested in discussing this, we would like to talk to you about this promotion and what role you might play in it (ultimately, it involves free airfare and hotel stay).

Sincerely and respectfully

Your fairy godmother
*(alias used to protect real identity)

HOLY CRAP!!!! DID THAT JUST HAPPEN?!

My jaw literally hit the floor.

So, for about 6 years, I've been a social media influencer, blogging on all things fashion, lifestyle, travel and more.

in·flu·encer:

Noun

a word Instagram users use to describe themselves to make them feel famous and important when no one really knows who they are or cares.

Because of this, I have had the privilege to work with some of the leading names in these industries, but this opportunity really takes the cake.

After screaming in disbelief and Googling if miracles are real, we were at the airport ready to board our all-paid-for flight to New York City before we could even blink.

Looking back on this time, it is clear as day that this all wouldn't have been possible without a little bit of prayer and a whole lot of manifestation.

God knows what we want and will always deliver if that is in *His plan*. The reason I speak of manifestation so highly is because I believe we are simply teaching ourselves to be optimistic again. When we experience a loss, we can become conditioned to believe that we aren't destined for happiness in the future. Negativity can be easily cemented in our brains if we don't proactively combat it.

But my New York miracle story keeps the positivity flowing for me. If it is in His will, He will make a way, especially when it feels like there is no way. Christ wants us to envision an abundant life for ourselves. In doing this, we are allowing ourselves to be ambitious, aspire, and dream.

Keep on asking and you will receive what you ask for. Keep on seeking and you will find. Keep on knocking and the door will be open for you (Matthew 7:7)

When I think of The Law of Attraction, it is us asking God for what we truly want and knowing that He will deliver it in the form that He has planned for us. So wherever you are and whatever you're going through, live your perfect life in your mind. Take away from what is at hand and encourage yourself to believe in what can be achieved. Train for the marathon, knowing God will get you all the way to the finish line.

So, say your prayers and manifest yourself to sleep tonight. Manifesting is your way of reassuring your heart and mind that you know you deserve greatness and will achieve it. Reveal to your mind what lies ahead.

Envision it today, live it tomorrow.

CHAPTER 15

Forgive All Parties

The most freeing thing in the world is also the most annoy-ing thing in the world. Yes, I am talking about forgiveness.

I am just going to put it out there that forgiving the ones who hurt us is a virtue I wish God didn't ask of us. It seems to be the one command of my faith that just takes too much of me. For the longest time I used to leave out the forgive part of the Lord's Prayer. I just couldn't bring myself to do that for the ones that burned me.

"...and forgive us our sins as we have forgiven those who sin against us" (Matthew 6:12)

What do you expect from a girl like me? I didn't have small troubles; I had the big lighting rod ones.

I went through all the normal troubles an average girl would go through, but, for me, they always went to the next, worst level.

Plenty of kids get bullied, which is never okay, but how many kids have girls put hair removal in their mascara to make their eyelashes fall off?

Lots of people get cheated on, but I hope they don't get cheated on with 8 other women.

It seemed like I always went through the "rite of passage" problems but ended up on the more severe side of it.

As a 25-year-old woman with no eyelashes and major trust issues, you can understand why forgiveness is not my strong suit.

I always wanted to be forgiven myself for my debts but didn't feel I was a big enough person to do it for my debtors. But no matter how I felt, I wouldn't be able to call myself a good Christian without pardoning the ones who have hurt me.

I was thinking about the ones that have lost my trust the other day. They all live in the same drawer in my mind. I couldn't help but think of all the unimaginable things each of these peo-ple had to have done to be completely shunned by a people-pleaser like me. It seemed I'd become a bitter person from not cleaning out that messy drawer. I knew it was time to do the adult thing and forgive my foes.

It wasn't easy, but what helped was knowing I could take pride in being the "bigger person" in all of this. If they needed an apology, they were going to get one. If they needed me to make the first move, I will. One by one, I released them and the memories once and for all.

In church, we're told to forgive, like it's easy, when actually it's one of the most challenging, emotional lessons of the hu-man journey. It takes a lot of guts and humility to master for-giveness. And sometimes, it seems pointless to even make that kind of effort. Why would we need to dig back through time and forgive others when they have no correlation to what we are dealing with at hand? To answer that question, it's because forgiveness is a skill you need to master. Forgiveness isn't really about the other person. It is about *you*.

Whether we're angry at someone else or ourselves, the ani-mosity we hold onto is equivalent to being stuck in quicksand. We can try to move forward and find our next path all we want, but if we don't know how to forgive, we will never get to our destination

Take it from me, the self-hatred bus is going nowhere good.

A couple of weeks ago I had to share a hotel room with my parents while we were traveling to visit some family. Although it was just for one night, I knew this would be complete torture. The thought of sharing a close space like that for 24 hours is not something I particularly was looking forward to. Sharing a small bathroom, unable to agree what to watch on TV, and absolutely no privacy was a recipe for disaster.

However, it wasn't what was going to happen while we were awake, but rather when we all go to sleep that would make this room situation even worse.

My parents are snorers! With both of them combined, the whole building could shake. What should have been a normal 8 hours of sleep turned into a night full of tossing and turning every hour while continuously checking the clock in hopes it was morning again. Even though I was in dire need of sleep, I couldn't wait for morning to come so I could get the heck out of that room.

As we were eating our breakfast the next morning in the hotel, I couldn't keep myself awake. There had been several times that I almost fell face first in my hot oatmeal. I wasn't able to function and when I tried, my emotions were all over the place. I felt easily agitated and impatient towards anything and anyone. It is no surprise that a lack of quality sleep can take a toll on a person's whole attitude the next day, and I was certainly proving that. As I was sitting there in my newfound irritated skin, something came to my mind.

Rewind to another time, I too also have a snoring problem. I guess the apple really doesn't fall far the tree. I feel we find out we snore in our older years of living, for it't not something that is brought to our attention at a very young age. But turns out, it was a problem I most definitely did have.

While living with my ex, you can expect that we shared a bedroom, and by the first night we had our first sleep in the apartment together, there was a less sexy reason *he didn't* get good sleep that night. Unfortunately, my snoring kept him awake all night. Come the first week of this it was full of "you know you snore, right?" "It is so cute you snore," "don't think I've ever met a girl that snores like you do." All comments were in a joking manner and for a while we just laughed at this little detail about our new relationship. But that didn't last long.

Since we lived together for almost 2 years, you can already assume that my snoring didn't magically disappear. My unintentional natural bodily function caused *him* to know what a slow burn of horrible quality of sleep can do to a person. Every day he became a more frustrated and stressed out person than the day before. He had very little patience and couldn't give his best to me or even himself. Lack of good sleep for almost 2 years seems almost unimaginable and unfortunately, I watched someone go through just that. Of course, I was aware enough to know this was a huge issue in our life and I did my very best to alleviate it as much as I could. I tried everything— nose strips, slept on my side, ear plugs for him, sleep studies, etc... but nothing worked. I still woke up in the middle of the night to find I was alone. In living together for so long, it might come as a shock we lasted in the same bed all night a handful of times. Intimacy went down the drain and it wasn't much longer until everything else did too. When our fighting began, it was always expressed that *his* horrible quality of sleep was to blame.

Better yet— I was to blame.

As I was sitting in the hotel lobby with my mom and dad, also dealing with an altered mood due to a bad night's sleep, I empathized with the same feelings I might have put someone else through. If I felt this on edge just after one night, I can't even imagine what all *he* felt.

Since we broke up very abruptly, my whole world changed, and sadly I didn't have many answers as to why. All I know was he ended up despising me and discarding me soon after. I can whole heartedly admit that I would do the same thing to my parents if I had to share another room with them ever again.

He had many faults and none of them correlated to my snoring, but in that moment I believed that was what knocked the first domino down.

If I didn't snore, he would have had more patience for us.

If I didn't snore, he wouldn't easily lash out.

If I didn't snore, he wouldn't feel the need to rely on other things to get him through the day.

If I didn't snore, he would've tried harder.

If I didn't snore, he would've never left.

If I didn't snore, my life would have never changed.

In these thoughts, I did what many women in emotionally and physically abusive relationships do. I started victim blaming and holding myself accountable for the downfall. There is a reason many women do this for it seems the only way we can feel content is when we have all the answers. And when we don't, we go down a spiral into creating false reasons that make sense to us. Was my snoring the catalyst that pushed everything else over the edge? Although it is a thought provoking question, it was the most unhealthy thing I could ever let in my mind.

Whether you did contribute to your own downfall or not, you still deserve to be pardoned for it. This feeling of adamantly wanting to place blame on myself threw me right back into the unhealthy cycle of our relationship, only it was just me there alone. *He* wasn't there but his words sure were. All the words of holding me in contempt of all that went wrong, for *he* was *apparently* perfect.

He was determined to place all the blame on me when things went south, and it is no shock I believed it all. Whether that was his easy way out to hurt me or how he actually felt, he made sure that I knew I was the root of all our problems during the relationship and after. When things don't go as planned, we experience all the emotions, but many of them are guilt, shame, and self-loathe, and we cannot help but point fingers at ourselves.

But when I realized that it was actually a case of a a narcissist being a narcissist, I knew what the truth was.

It was then that I had to forgive myself for placing any sort of blame on myself in the first place. It was time for me to release my thoughts and stop believing that I would still be with that man if I had been a better, sound sleeper of a woman. There will be times in your journey where you will be prompted with questions like these. You will have feelings and premonitions of what you feel you could have done differently. And reader, that is not a wrong feeling to wonder. However, once you act on that feeling believing that if you did something different your outcome would have been different too is not healthy. If your love or even a job doesn't value you, don't believe that you are the one to blame for their actions towards you. Before this realization, I would up every day think *sure it was bad back where I was, but I would trade it for what I am going through now.* The feeling of being alone, empty, and heartbroken seemed like a prize over my current circumstances. It is a feeling we all try to admit we don't have, but in reality, we have all gone through the bargaining stage in times like these. Unfortunately, we end up doing more harm than good when we keep looking in the rear-view mirror of our life.

After constantly repeating to myself how much I would exchange what I have now for what I used to have, I soon started to believe myself. As the days and months went by, and I should have been getting stronger, I was feeling more defeated each day. With all the sadness came the hurt, anger, and even rage. But who could I blame for feeling this way? As time went on, my ex's memory became very faint and I wasn't able to draw from instances that led me to leave him at all. The rage had to come out, but the one person I should and could've put that on was not around anymore. The only other person involved that was still around was *me*.

In quiet times and even the loud ones too, I was able to pull from every off-putting thing my ex said to me. All the comments about being dependent to even just not wanting to speak to me at all because he was too high to remember what planet he was on, were all that replayed in my mind for months.

To an outsider, those comments are helpful when reminding someone what they dodged and why they left, but to me, it was these very comments that turned the blame inward and made me feel disgusted to be who I am. A recommendation that I found in times I shifted blame easily was to label the ones who brought you into this journey. If you are dealing with an ex-love, write out a list of all that they did and said that were wrong, disrespectful, and created a bad energy within your relationship. When your mind wants to go into guilt you can pull out your handy-dandy notes to speak logic that you might not be able to do for yourself.

It is not hard to hold ourselves guilty to another person's actions, especially when they spend much time creating comments that make you feel you were the problem all along. If we do not get the accountability we feel we deserve from someone else, we soon believe maybe we are the ones who created this mess.

I figured out why I had been stuck in quicksand. I knew what had been preventing me from moving forward. Sure, I was going through all the right motions. I was going to therapy and taking medication for my mental health. I worked out daily and meditated any chance I got. Essential oils, mood journals, vision boards, you name it! I was doing it all. But I still felt stuck.

I soon grasped that I had been not only holding onto my past but holding myself in contempt for it too. I realized it was time to forgive myself and *him*, for my own sake. I didn't deserve to feel that way and have those thoughts. I deserved to be free to move forward.

That's what forgiveness really is: freedom.

Become free of your past and the thoughts that want to keep you there. We are not perfect, and none of us is without blame. Whether we're the ones who have caused our lives to go haywire or not, forgiveness is the answer. As hard as it may seem to forgive others, it takes even more strength to be the "bigger person" for yourself. Forgiving yourself can be different for everyone. For me, I forgave myself for loving someone who didn't treat me the way I deserved to be treated. After that, it didn't seem quite so big a deal to forgive him. I hope that you can find the same freedom through forgiveness. It requires empathy, compassion, patience, and understanding. By choosing to forgive, you are keeping love for yourself at the forefront. Let your love for yourself be more important than any anger, hurt or blame you might feel, towards yourself or anyone else. Forgive, let go of the past, and be free to enjoy what's next.

Don't put yourself in the hotseat after you were told you could have been better woman. Brush it off your shoulder and start to move forward. If you hold any hostility towards yourself you cannot better yourself and find what is yet to come.

After all, isn't that what they wanted to do to us all along? We just cracked their code.

CHAPTER 16

We Were Made to Thrive

As human beings, we tend to confuse our wants and our needs. Somedays I feel like I *want* water and *need* Instagram followers. I crosswire them all the time.

Apparently, what we actually need are air, water, food, shelter, and clothing.

Great, that means I must *need* that cute sweater I've been eyeing up at Target!

I kid. Sort of. But not really. Because the truth is I might be able to survive on just the basics, but I wouldn't be *me*.

If life was made up of just meeting our needs, then life would be pretty boring.

I believe our purpose in life is to achieve far more than the basics. We are built to strive for more than just the essentials. It's our will to live, to turn our passions into purpose, into success.

This kind of happiness is what makes life fruitful and vibrant. Dreams that turn to reality is what we call a success story. Now, you and I have just lived through the opposite of that.

If the words above like "passion," "purpose," and "success" are giving you massive anxiety, you are not alone. Although I talk big about the basics not being enough, there was a time when they were all I was capable of.

For a while, my life consisted of the bare minimum. I would wake up, do the same mundane and unfulfilling job every day, eat and drink to keep my organs functioning, brush my teeth to keep them from rotting, go to bed, and repeat the next day.

Although this kind of existence seems like complete torture, it felt like the only life I could actually live after my life fell apart. No expectations, no responsibilities, no potential heartbreaks in the future. It was the simple life I had no idea I would be so attracted to.

I used to have so many reasons to jump out of bed every morning. I was filled with more ambition than Dolly's cup and knew that life was only getting better for me. Of course, I still went through life's challenges, but never anything I couldn't work through. I believed I could do anything. My plans were aligning with my timing, my hard work was paying off, and, best of all, I didn't have a global pandemic causing the world to ground to a halt. The world was my oyster. But it soon became more like an empty seafood buffet when it all disappeared.

I used to get up thinking, what amazing things would I accomplish today? But post-breakup the only thoughts that came to mind were "If I lay low enough today, nothing can hurt me."

I lived the bare minimum life for so long that even watching other people surpass me in their own life didn't affect me the way it previously would have.

I was surviving, but I wasn't really *living*.

I wasn't experiencing life in the way God intended for me to, with courage, hope, dreams, guts, power, and fortune. Is it possible we can't survive without our *wants* to?

We can fool ourselves, to an extent, that we want to live a simple life, but we can only act that way for so long. After three months of merely existing, I became restless with knowing it was time to become more than just a body again.

I went to the drawing board to really find out what I wanted to see happen in my life, and how I could make it happen. Who did I want to be? What would I want to achieve? How could I live a life that is worth living? I mean isn't this that what finding our Plan B really is? What is Plan B to you? Is it the same life you had before, just with the right person or situation, or is it something you never had the time or ability to do until now?

What do you *want*? And I'm talking deathbed want here. What will ensure that, when you die, you die fulfilled and content? Do you want something tangible? A flashy car? A home to call your own? Or do you desire something money can't buy? A happy marriage and family?

We only get one life, and we deserve to do more than survive.

We were meant to thrive.

To take the one life we've been given and become our most beautiful, authentic selves that **God put us on this Earth to be.**

This is the time to let go and let God, because there is in fact so much more He has promised for you. He has promised a purposeful life, and, whether or not you believe me, you have a purpose.

As I started thinking about this, I remembered a few people in my own life who have given up on their faith and missed out on the search for their purpose. Each of them has gone through their own struggles and have had to face many hard challenges. As time went on, they started to rely on their own understanding more, rather than God's. Each struggle they encountered was looked at more so like a punishment rather than a lesson. So far they've refused to learn and let God in, but I know that He holds patience and grace towards them for whenever they decide to come back home to Him.

I am here to tell you that you cannot thrive without God. He carries the blueprint of your life, so locking Him out would not be to your benefit. We cannot move forward without God's presence all around us. To eat, sleep, and breathe the Lord is how he made us and wants us to live. Especially when your whole world is unrecognizable, He is working towards something so much greater for us. Something we will not understand until it is revealed, and, when it is, it will be through God's timing.

"No eye has seen, no ear has heard, and no mind has imagined what God has prepared for those who love him." (1 Corinthians 2:9)

Whatever you've had to say goodbye to, whatever life you never imagined not living, only goes to show how amazing your life that is yet to come will be. How awesome is that!?

That is the definition of Plan B.

We are looking to God for our Plan B, because He holds the passcode to unlock it. Plan B has been God's Plan A for us all along. He knows what we *want*, but, better yet, he knows what we *need*.

I started thinking, maybe things don't go as planned for God to show us that <u>He is the plan.</u>

Now, I am not saying that God was ever meant to be our next best. He is not an afterthought. He is never meant to be the person we run to after something goes awry. Sadly, it is when things do go bad that we start to seek Him out. I am extremely guilty of this.

We are being asked to draw near to Him. To not make any decisions without including Him in every single one. To heal and recover with Him by our side. To perform any daily tasks with his help, to cook, clean, drive the car, leave the house, and anything else your days consist of—He wants to be a part of it all. Your Plan B is His Plan A-Z. He has wanted all of you from the start, over and over. Every time we slip away, He still wants you like it's the first time. If we knew someone on this Earth who acts the same way, they would be considered forgiving to a fault. This reckless kind of love is the best blessing we as flawed human beings could ever receive.

Allow this to be a constant reminder to never stray away from Him again. But if you do, He will open His arms wide open every time.

This is what it means to *thrive*. We were made for more than an ordinary life, and God wants that for us. To have a far-from-ordinary life is one lived through Christ. He can teach us things that we never knew before. He can take us places we never dreamt of going. He can provide abundance bigger than we ever wished for. You cannot thrive without Him by your side.

Knowledge of our Father is what might have been missing while you were drawing out your Plan A, and that is ok. He will not fault you because He was not included the first time, but this is your do-over to include Him now.

After speaking with God, I found out what I have been avoiding to admit.

I had fallen into the trap of idolatry and false faith. I had given so much power to my future instead of living peacefully in my present. Whether it was love for a person or thing, it took precedent over God every time. In losing what I lost, I gained a stronger bond with God. He is a giving and taking God, for both actions create a purpose for us and a stronger understanding in Him.

You are still here and alive to enter into what is yet to come. To be able to grab God by the hand, put your big girl boots on, and go forward is what makes you a survivor. Sorry, a *thriver*. You thrive even at your worst when you decide to still give it your best. Thriving doesn't mean that you must have something show for it. You don't need a prize, title, money, family, love, etc... You need God.

You were made by Him, and He made you to *thrive*.

CHAPTER 17

Look at Her Now

Alright everyone, we've reached the homestretch, and this is the moment you've been waiting for. The moment when I give you the scientific, fool-proof formula for figuring out what your Plan B is!

Ha. Jokes.

But seriously, all that we have been training for has led us to this moment, and it is time to start putting one foot in front of the other again.

We aren't nearing the end of our journey, but we have picked up some very useful tips to ease the trip. I believe that calling this a journey really solidifies what it means to find your Plan B. It is less about what you find and more about how you find it. And even more so, it is how you handle it.

After all, nothing you go through will ever define you. What does is your reaction.

Now, I know I am saying some pretty basic Home Good's wall art quotes, but, hey, they're mass-produced because they're true.

I have always been an overreacting person when it comes to situations not panning out correctly. Jumping to conclusions, getting heated very quickly, and sometimes saying the wrong thing out of anger, I've ended up doing more harm than good over the years. And creating a world of embarrassment for myself afterwards.

After all, the world is full of eyes watching your every move, in person and through their screens. Knowing that you're being examined on your good days as well as your bad ones really pushes us to be on our best behavior at all times.

When my whole world fell apart and it was time to pick up the pieces, I kept feeling a sense of embarrassment. I was a girl who got out of her hometown, moved to the big city, got a great job, fell in love, just to lose it all in the blink of an eye. My dirty laundry was on display due to my big presence on social media and my gigantic family. I have never been afforded much privacy in my life, and, come to think of it, that might explain a lot.

All I know is many people were curious when I stopped sharing all of my day-to-day expeditions. There were no pictures of *him* or my beloved city anymore, and people took notice.

I'd moved away from my hometown to make a name for myself. I wanted to get out and enjoy the big city life and all its' opportunities. People knew I was getting out and were super proud of me. Heck, even my hometown bullies took notice. Several of them had even called me to say they were sorry for all the hurt they caused and to congratulate me on my new adventures.

But when it all fell down, what did they have to say about me then?

"She thought she could have it all. HA! *Look at her now.*"

Not only was I hard on myself, but I was suddenly thinking about all the other people who might be hard on me in this season too.

Look at me now.

What do I have to show for after this turn of events?

Just last week my dad and I decided to walk the trail at our local park. Since the construction company he works for built all the park amenities, I felt like I was walking with a tour guide rather than my dad. He had so many pieces of useless information about everything we passed by. The whole time I wanted to scream, "Ok dad! I don't care that much about walkway lamp posts."

While we were taking our stroll, I noticed I had my credit card still in my back pocket from lunch. I asked my dad to hold on to my card until we got back in the car. Once we got back in the car, the first thing I did was ask for my card back. As I started to watch him search and scramble through his retro dad windbreakers, I knew what had just happened. He'd lost my card somewhere in the middle of a 185-acre park. I noticed his confusion go into panic very quickly. I am not sure if you were blessed like me with the most caring man in the whole world for a dad, but I could see he felt like losing my credit card was a monumental disappointment. My dad is the type of person who wants to be relied on. He takes pride in being an attentive parent, brother, employee, and friend. So, when he misplaced my card, I could tell he wasn't used to letting people down and felt really bad.

It wasn't long after the panic that I realized he wasn't going to find my credit card and it was time for me to react.

When thinking about how I normally respond to situations that go south, it seems I am a hot head. My natural reaction would have been to point out how thoughtless and careless he had been. With all of the stress that I had been put under lately, I could not afford the slightest hiccup in the road. But in that moment, I decided to take a different route for once.

I turned to my dad, put on a big smile, and said "It's ok, Dad. Don't worry about it. Things happen." I was uttering these words while adding a slight chuckle, encouraging him to laugh at the circumstances with me.

When I did that, it still took him a minute to brush it off his shoulder, but after creating a more positive environment, he started to believe in my reassurance.

After re-walking the park just to look for my credit card, I started to wonder if God was trying to sneak in another much-needed workout.

Once it was clear we weren't going to find it, I did call and cancel the card. The end.

The reason I shared this story is because of what happened after.

When we returned home my mom asked how our walk went. I heard my dad in the other room talking about the weather and such, but then I overheard him tell my mom how he had lost my card in the park, and how we had turned a 20-minute walk into an hour-long scavenger hunt. But then I heard my dad say this: "Although I lost her credit card, she was great. She remained calm the whole time and made me feel better about the whole thing."

That was a moment that really stood out to me. People will tend to forget what has happened in your life, but they will never forget how you handled it. In remaining calm, I achieved way more than I would have if I'd jumped to anger and despair. By allowing myself to remain positive and calm, I was able to imprint a good feeling on my dad.

This is what I want to be known for. I could be known as the girl whose whole life turned upside down, leaving me embarrassed, hurt, and damaged. Or I could be known as the girl who triumphed through the hardships while remaining hopeful, positive, and resilient.

I had a choice to make, and, my friend, you do too.

What do you want people to think of when they hear your name?

After I heard what my dad had to say about my reaction to the scene, I felt a sense of accomplishment. It felt as if it was a rewarding moment that I had been working on to get right for so long. I left a mark on someone, but more importantly, I left a mark on myself. It was in that moment that I knew that was the feeling I always wanted to achieve.

To acquire a legacy and lead by example is who I want to be, but no one ever earned those titles by taking the easy road. It takes going to Hell and back to gain that type of notoriety from others. To think, how would we be able to describe some of the most inspiring people of our time, without them having to overcome some form adversity?

Finding your Plan B isn't about what the Plan B is; it is about the journey you take to find it. You are becoming a person who is capable of creating their Plan B. You are ready to take on that challenge. After all, your next endeavor will have more meaning because it took a world full of effort and determination to achieve it. Your happiness will mean more and will be protected at all costs, because you know what it is like to not be at your absolute best.

After this is all said and done, you and I could have it all.

I knew that my demeanor throughout this whole process had become much more important than really finding out what lay ahead. I wanted to be seen for the resilient, positive, and overcoming woman that I was shaping out to be.

I not only want your Plan B to be successful, but I hope you find many successes along the way to finding it. I want you to seriously take a moment and be proud of not only coming this far in the book but coming this far in your journey. By getting through this book, you are achieving so much in a time where you could be questioning how it is possible to achieve anything at all. The little achievements are so much more than you ever thought.

Rising up can be your Plan B in itself. The ability to walk out of the dark still standing is an accomplishment of its' own, and there are many people who are still longing to do the same in their own lives. The fact that you are able to take this step in wanting to put your past behind you and build something even better already makes you 10x more resilient than you were before. Don't let finding your Plan B only become something worth celebrating once it is found. Success isn't just what you receive, it is the battle you fight to earn it. The small successes need to be treated like the big ones, for you were once in a state where the small tasks were the hardest to undertake.

This is a comeback to be remembered. After all, how memorable are the ones who took the easy road? The ones who had everything handed to them? But we weren't on the road most traveled on. Ours is a road of pure hope, prayers, and maybe even the good ole blood, sweat, and tears, and that's why we *will* turn our truest hopes and dreams into a reality.

This is a revival. God is using you right now to shape you into the woman He made you to be. Losing your dreams might have come as a shock to you, but it was all in the fine print that God had all along in His plans for you.

So know this:

In a world of questions, there are answers.
In a world of blindness, there is a vision.
In a world of bondage there is a freedom

I hope you fall in love with your journey. This time in your life is shaping you into the person you were put on this Earth to be. Without the circumstances that led you to this point, you would have never had the chance to be this woman in all her form and glory. You are becoming a person full of power because you know what it feels like to be powerless. You are now protecting yourself at all costs and setting boundaries to guard the new and improved outlook you have. After all, our Plan B is greater than what stood before, so there should only be excitement and anticipation from here on out. I am just as ready for your life to fall back into place as you are. I am here to call you out of the dark! To reset your broken heart into a vessel stronger than you have ever known before. Break down those prison walls and forge ahead without getting lost looking in the rearview mirror. There might still be pain, and that is ok. Pain is beautiful in its own way, for it can gift you with creativity. Get excited to tell your story the way I have done and speak about it as a blessing rather than a curse. Become your story, and your purpose will be revealed.

Just remember this: what brought you on this journey doesn't matter. All that does is how you rise.

Look at you now!

Notes

Introduction

Rosner, E., 2020. *US divorce rates skyrocket amid COVID-19 pandemic.* [online] New York Post. Available at: <https://nypost.com/2020/09/01/divorce-rates-skyrocket-in-u-s-amid-covid-19/>.

Expectations vs Reality

Legally Blonde. 2001. [film] Directed by R. Luketic. Los Angeles: Metro-Goldwyn-Mayer.

Ugh, God

(NLT, Job 1:21)

(NLT, Job 30:20-22)

The "C" Word

(NLT, Matthew 6:8)

~~Love~~ Validate Yourself

Loannidou, F. and Konstantikaki, V., 2008. Empathy and emotional intelligence: What is it really about? *International Journal of Caring Sciences*, [online] 1(3), p.120. Available at: <http://international-journalofcaringsciences.org/docs/Vol1_Issue3_03_Ioannidou.pdf>

The Only Way Out Is Through

Malcolm, X., 2016. *Trypanophobia - A Fear of Needles - Health Beat*. [online] Available at: https://jamaicahospital.org/newsletter/trypano-phobia -a-fear-of-needles/>.

GET ANGRY

(NLT, Romans 12:2)

Its Not Ok to be Ok

"The One In Massapequa." *Friends*. Created by David Crane, Marta Kauffman, Kevin Bright, season 8, episode 18. Warner Brothers Television Distribution, 2002.

Unplug

Lally, P., van Jaarsveld, C., Potts, H. and Wardle, J., 2009. How are habits formed: Modelling habit formation in the real world. *European Journal of Social Psychology*, 40(6), p.998.

Take Out The Trash

(NLT, 2 Corinthians 11:14)

Baby, I Can Be Your Motivation

Kolk, B., 2000. Posttraumatic stress disorder and the nature of
trauma. *Posttraumatic Stress Disorder*, 2(1), pp.7-22.

(NLT, Proverbs 4:25)

Feeling Gratitude

(NLT, James 1:17)

Babakhan, J., n.d. *Twists of fate that saved these people's lives on 9/11.*
[online] Reader's Digest Asia. Available at: <https://www.rdasia.com/
culture/twists-of-fate-that-saved-these-peoples-lives-on-9-11>

Manifest It

(NLT, Matthew 7:12)

Forgive All Parties

(NLT, Matthew 6:12)

We Were Made to Thrive

(NLT, 1 Corinthians 2:9)

About the Author

Tala Shatara, author of her first book, *Finding Plan B*, is no stranger to the world of writing. Born and raised in East Tennessee, Tala went on to study at the University of Tennessee, Knoxville majoring in Journalism and Electronic Media. With her interests in writing starting out very young, Tala went on to win multiple awards that showcased her writing skills. Due to her time at the University of Tennessee, Tala also spent time in the world of broadcast journalism. Tala has experience reporting local, entertainment and sports news.

Tala is also a freelance blogger. She shares on all things fashion, travel, and lifestyle. She has represented big names like American Airlines, Mercedes Benz, and Uber. Being an entrepreneur herself, Tala also spent some time mentoring other entrepreneurs that have interest in branding themselves online. Tala created Knoxville's first ever TrendFest. This event allows aspiring and established social creatives to get connected and become inspired.

Tala takes pride in her Palestinian heritage and helps organize events that showcase East Tennessee's growing Arab-American population. She is outspoken about Palestinian rights and their humanity. Tala has raised several funds that help the children of Palestine who are facing violence and abuse.

Tala also has also spent time working in the music industry helping songwriters collect royalties for their work. While living in Nashville, Tala helps business owners obtain copyright permission for the public performance of songwriter's music.

Tala isn't stopping here and plans to continue on with her writing.

Follow along with Tala!

@talashatara

talashatara.com